OUT OF THE BOX

BUILDING ROBOTS, TRANSFORMING LIVES

OUT OF THE BOX
BUILDING ROBOTS, TRANSFORMING LIVES

ANDREW B. WILLIAMS, PH.D.
Founder of the First All-Female RoboCup Team

and Edward Gilbreath

MOODY PUBLISHERS
CHICAGO

All Scripture quotations, unless otherwise indicated, are taken from *The New American Standard Bible*®, Copyright © 1960, 1962, 1963, 1968, 1971, 1972, 1973, 1975, 1977, 1995 by The Lockman Foundation. Used by permission. (www.lockman.org)

All Scripture quotations, unless otherwise indicated, are taken from the *Holy Bible, New International Version*®. NIV®. Copyright © 1973, 1978, 1984 by International Bible Society. Used by permission of Zondervan. All rights reserved.

Scripture quotations marked KJV are taken from the King James Version.

Cover Design: Trevell Southhall
Cover Image: Rick Cash
Cd Cover Design: TS Design Studio
Interior Design: Ragont Design

Library of Congress Cataloging-in-Publication Data

Williams, Andrew B.
  Out of the box : building robots, transforming lives / Andrew B. Williams, with Edward Gilbreath.
    p. cm.
  ISBN 978-0-8024-6760-7
  1. Williams, Andrew B. 2. Christian biography. 3. Robotics—United States—Biography. 4. African American women.
  5. Robotics—Vocational guidance. 6. Vocation—Christianity.
  I. Gilbreath, Edward, 1969- II. Title.

BR1725.W4545A3 2009
277.3'083092—dc22
[B]
                                          2008037266

1 3 5 7 9 10 8 6 4 2

Printed in the United States of America

To my loyal, loving wife, Anitra,
"I love you forever."
To our children, John, Adrianna,
and Rosa, "You are our greatest treasures."
And to my parents, John and Yuson Williams

"Talent can come from anywhere."
—SPIKE LEE

"But God chose the foolish things of the world to shame the wise; God chose the weak things of the world to shame the strong."
—PAUL, THE APOSTLE

Contents

FOREWORD

Several months before Barack Obama became the first African American president of the United States of America, I stood in the pulpit of our church in historic College Park, Georgia, and introduced a young tenured professor at Spelman College named Dr. Andrew B. Williams. I felt so proud. Proud because the inspiration and hope that the fulfillment of his dream gives to the young men and women in our College Park community is no less equal to the inspiration and hope the fulfillment of Barack Obama's dream of becoming president gives to young men and women of color throughout the world.

While *Out of the Box* is a story that will surely inspire and give hope to many in pursuit of their dreams, it's actually more than that. It's a fresh testimony of God's ability to translate dreams into reality and affirms the Scripture that teaches the immutability of God and that He's no respecter of persons. What He did for Joseph in Egypt, He does for a kid named Drew. What He did for a kid named Drew, He can also do for me and you.

But—as *Out of the Box* demonstrates, it doesn't all just happen automatically! True, some dreams do "dry up," "fester," or "stink like rotten meat." Others "crust and sugar over like syrupy sweet." Still some "sag like a heavy load" and for sure others do "explode" as Langston Hughes says. But perhaps the reasons so many dreams are deferred has more to do with the internal courage to continue pursuit of them than external forces eager to hinder them. One thing that is made clear over and over in this well written book (which by the way reveals that Dr. Williams is as much a story teller as he is a scientist) is that "It's courage that counts." You'll notice that if it had not been for the courage he displays in exercising his faith, loving his family and trusting God with his future, at any juncture, his life could have easily chartered a different course.

Honestly, I don't think God would have it any other way—than to require us to demonstrate courage. When we do, particularly when the odds are against us, as they were for Dr. Williams, more glory goes to Him. In other words, the greater the odds, the greater the glory!

Robert Crummie
Pastor, Mount Calvary Missionary Baptist Church
President, Carver Bible College
College Park, Georgia

ACKNOWLEDGMENTS

I want to first thank my beautiful and godly wife, Anitra, who has loved and supported me faithfully for the last sixteen plus years. She is my greatest friend, counselor and encourager and without her I would not have been able to write this book. My children, John, Adrianna, and Rosa are my greatest treasures and inspire me to be a trailblazer for their futures. My Mom, Yuson Kim Williams, and Dad, John Morgan Williams, who loved us and served as great role models of parents who worked hard to provide for their children in the most challenging of circumstances. My brothers and sisters, Dr. Robert Williams, Jeanne Delaney, Morgan Williams, Mary Neal, and George Williams, were and continue to be my role models and best cheerleaders.

I am thankful for Edward Gilbreath, for helping me to find a voice and write my personal story in an engaging manner. I am thankful for all those at the Institute for Black Family Development and Moody Publishers, including Matthew Parker, Karen Waddles and Greg Thornton, who believed in this story enough to publish it for the Lift Every Voice imprint. I want to thank Dr. Larry Mercer who first heard my story and encouraged me to write it with Moody and made the connections for me along with my pastor and friend, Rev. Robert Crummie.

Spelman College entrusted me with some of her students to teach and seek to inspire, and for that I am grateful. I want to acknowledge all those at Spelman College including President Beverly Daniel Tatum, Provost Johnnella Butler, Associate Provost of Research Lily McNair, Dr. Andrea Lawrence, and my colleagues in the Computer and Information Sciences department for their support and advice. Without President Tatum, our SpelBots would not have been able to compete.

I am particularly grateful for the countless hours that Mike Jordahl and Pastor Leo Barbee Jr. discipled, counseled, and shared their lives with me during my college years at KU and helped set the positive direction for my adult life. I am convinced that my family and I would not have made it had not it been for the families from our church in Junction City, Kansas, including David and Sharon Scoggins, Warren and Georgia Martin, Merle Fawley, and Juanita Schwab.

I have many other mentors, colleagues, and role models to thank including Pastor Leroy Armstrong, Pastor Charles Briscoe, Pastor James Carrington, Pastor Terrill Worthington, Pastor Jesse Bradley, Pastor Orlando Dial, Michael Shinn, Dr. Bill Hogan, Dean Carl Locke, Associate Dean Thomas Mulinazzi, Florence Boldridge, Dean Stanley Jaskolski, Dr. Tom Casavant, Dr. Edwin Stone, Dr. Costas Tsatsoulis, Dr. M. Brian Blake, Dr. Ayanna Howard, Dr. Juan Gilbert, Dr. James Heinen, Dr. David Touretzky, Tony and Lauren Dungy, Carey and Melanie Casey, Pastor Ray and Robin McKelvy, Antoine Lawrence, Richawn Buford, Dr. Ronald and Rhonda Moore, Dr. Ken Demarest, Jeff Huskerson, Tony Gatewood, Denise Young-Smith, Scott Gilfoil, and all my school teachers from Washington Elementary School, Junction City Junior High School, and Junction City High School.

I am also grateful to those early sponsors of our SpelBots including The Coca-Cola Foundation, NASA, Boeing, GE, Ted Aronson, and the National Science Foundation.

I also want to thank the original SpelBots, Aryen Moore-Alston, Brandy Kinlaw, Shinese Noble, Ebony Smith, Ebony O'Neal, and Karina Liles as well as all of the SpelBots that followed because they are the real heroes of my story because of the barriers they are helping to break.

And finally, I am the most grateful to the one true God who has made Himself real to me in the person of Jesus Christ, to whom I give all the glory for what He is doing in and through my life. Psalm 115:1.

"It's Courage That Counts"

When I tell some people I teach at a historically black college, it elicits polite nods. When I tell them I teach at a historically black women's college, some eyebrows may arch. When I tell them I teach students at a historically black women's college how to program robotic canines to compete in international soccer tournaments, their eyes bulge and they want to know more.

I arrived in Atlanta, Georgia, in 2004 to teach computer science at Spelman College. After years at predominantly white universities, I had answered the call to join the faculty of an HBCU (Historically Black College and University). I knew before I got there that launching an extracurricular robotics team to get young African American women interested in artificial intelligence and other areas of computer technology would be one of my top goals.

I started from scratch, quietly scouting and recruiting students from my various classes and contacts. Whenever I had the chance, I did my best salesman's pitch. I extolled the thrill and excitement of working with artificial intelligence and giving life and purpose to otherwise inanimate objects. I showed sample robot dog dances, demonstrating the fun they could have programming the Sony

AIBO[1] canines that are used in robotics competitions.

I hoped that my passion for education would be contagious, that it would pique the curiosity of enough committed students to make the robotics team more than just a professor's wild dream. I shared with them the quote by Winston Churchill that had driven my quest for academic, professional, and personal achievement: "Success is never final. Failure is seldom fatal. But it's courage that counts."

And I prayed.

I prayed both for the students whom God would inspire to be a part of the team, and for myself—that my motives and ambition would be unselfish and true.

Finally, after weeks of grassroots campaigning, my prayers were answered. Six bright and adventurous young women made the commitment to form Spelman's first robotics club. The SpelBots— Aryen Moore-Alston, Brandy Kinlaw, Shinese Noble, Ebony Smith, Ebony O'Neal, and Karina Liles—were born.

They hailed from diverse backgrounds and situations. They came from urban, suburban, and rural communities. Some of them came from families of college graduates; others were the first in their families to attend college. Some came from two-parent homes and some from single-parent homes. Though their journeys to Spelman varied, they each had something in common. They each lived in a world where women were severely underrepresented in the field of computer science, especially robotics. They each lived in a society that told them women could not excel at science and mathematics. (And I won't even bother going into what the world had to say to them as *black* women.)

As I watched the SpelBot team members grow in their enthu-siasm for robotics, I searched for ways to keep them increasingly challenged. I enjoyed watching them develop an affectionate rap-port with the cute AIBO robots that Spelman had purchased for the computer science department.

The Sony AIBO, which looks like a mechanical puppy, under-stands and responds to more than a hundred words and phrases when loaded with its preprogrammed AI (artificial intelligence) memory stick. The creature also sits, lies down, rights itself, and uses its face, tails, ears, and sounds to express emotion. At a cost of $2,000 per robot, the AIBO is embraced by academic artificial-intelligence researchers because it represents the latest in robotic technology—and it's relatively affordable. Our challenge was to reprogram these robots to "teach" them to play "four-on-four" robot soccer on a green-carpeted soccer field with color-coded markers and soccer goals.

Even before several weeks of mastering robot-programming fundamentals with the help of some robotics workshops given by Carnegie Mellon University, I suggested they'd get more programming experience by entering their robots in the RoboCup soccer competition. The SpelBots were both excited and nervous about the prospects of the competition. They were also motivated by the prospect of traveling across the ocean to Japan to compete.

During the school year, the SpelBots team members spent several hours each week programming and training their four robots in preparation for the U.S. RoboCup national competition at the end of the school year. The 2005 U.S. RoboCup was held in May, just down the road from Spelman at Georgia Tech.

A bit anxious and intimidated about going up against the more experienced graduate students that comprised our competition—plus having just faced final exams the week prior to the tournament—the girls persevered. And in the process, they became the first all-female team, and the first team representing an HBCU to compete in a RoboCup. Needless to say, I was quite proud of them.

Fast-forward two months to July 2005, and to the SpelBots on the world stage of robotics technology, competing at the international RoboCup tournament in Osaka, Japan. In less than a year, these six outstanding young women had ridden their curiosity, intellect, and tenacity to the highest level of competition in the field of artificial intelligence and computer technology. And in doing so, they made history.

When people ask me why I would come to Spelman from a Big

Ten major research institution, all I have to do is point them to these six young women, as well as the students who would follow them.

In truth, my journey to Spelman was a spiritual one. After reading Rick Warren's bestseller *The Purpose-Driven Life*, I decided that one reason God made me was to uplift and enable African American young people academically, vocationally, spiritually, and economically.

I want the world to know what is possible when we inspire our young women and men to dream beyond themselves—dream seemingly impossible dreams that become possible when you believe in a Creator much bigger than yourself.

In a very real way, their story is my story.

Before I received a master's degree in computer engineering and a Ph.D. in electrical engineering; before I became a recognized scholar in the field of distributed artificial intelligence, autonomous agents and multiagent systems, educational robotics and bioinformatics (which is a fancy way of saying I'm a hopeless computer geek); before I made professional connections with high-profile institutions such as the National Science Foundation, NASA, Microsoft Research, and Apple Inc.; before any of this I was a poor, biracial child from a Kansas ghetto whom society, for all intents and purposes, had written off.

Yet, here I am. And why? Because of the stubborn love, commitment, and prayers of faithful men and women whom God placed in my life along the way, including my African American Dad and my Korean Mom and my five siblings who were my first role models and mentors.

This book is a story about robots and artificial intelligence and the joy of education. But before that, it's a book about family, love, perseverance, and faith. It's about believing in the potential of every human being created in the image of God, despite their upbringing or societal status. It's a book about finding and pursuing our unique calling, even when it doesn't make sense. It's about not letting others define your destiny by putting you in a "box" of low expectations, or putting God in a "box" of limitations and excuses.

You'll see Churchill's quote invoked a few times throughout these pages—"Success is never final. Failure is seldom fatal. But it's courage that counts." Not only is it one of my favorite maxims; it has become God's reminder to me about what it takes to follow Him— academically, vocationally, spiritually. I hope my story of overcoming life's odds to build robots and impact lives will speak to yours.

CHAPTER 1

God Don't Make No Junk, Even in Junk City

For someone who has spent most of his adult life trying to think outside the box, it's weird for me to think that I spent the earliest days of my life in a cardboard box. My Korean-born mother, Yuson Kim-Williams, used to tell me the story of how she'd lay me to sleep in a small box because our family couldn't afford a baby crib.

In a sense, boxes defined my early upbringing. My African American dad, John Morgan Williams, left the Army around the time of my birth in 1964 and bought a box-shaped, two-bedroom trailer on Grant Avenue in Junction City, Kansas, known as "Junk City" to some. All six Williams kids somehow lived, played, and slept in that tiny square trailer.

Junk City was adjacent to Fort Riley, Kansas, the home of Fort Riley, where my dad was stationed by the Army after the Korean War. Fort Riley served as headquarters of the Big Red One 1st Infantry Division. At that time, Fort Riley also was unofficially designated as a "compassionate fort"—an Army base where many of the interracial couples were assigned, in part to protect them from the prejudice that existed in the wider society.

Many soldiers had met their spouses in either Asia or Europe during the different wars, which led to a boom in interracial marriages. So it wasn't that unusual for me, growing up, to see families that were black and white, white and Asian, and even black and Asian, like my family. According to my dad, in those days the military would send interracial families to compassion bases so they'd be in a community with other interracial families. Because of this, I knew other kids that looked like me. And so, for many years I was sheltered from some of the harsh realities of the outside world. I thought that growing up in a small Kansas town with black and Asian parents wasn't so unusual. Of course, as time passed, I came to understand how unusual we were in the broader landscape of small-town Kansas.

Seoul Connections

Prior to settling down in Junction City, Dad went back to Seoul, Korea, to bring home Momma and my older siblings—Momma's son, Robert, from a previous relationship, and Dad and Mom's wedlocked children, Jeanne and Morgan. My sister Jeanne still remembers how Korean children mocked her for being born to a black American soldier. She and Morgan were rescued from some of that ridicule when Dad returned to Korea to marry Mom and bring his new family to America.

My parents never talked about the details of their courtship. All we knew was that they met in Seoul, quickly fell in love, and began a risky affair. After finishing up his tour in Korea, Dad could've returned home and forgotten about my mother and my older siblings, as many returning soldiers had done. Instead, he knew it was his duty to go back and take care of his family. My father wasn't a Christian at the time, but I like to think he was motivated by a God-inspired love for Mom, Robert, Jeanne, and Morgan.

A Loving Family

Dad never told me why he didn't go back to settle in his hometown of Ansonia, Connecticut, after his military service. He visited there with his new family upon returning from Korea but would ultimately decide to make Kansas his permanent home. Consequently, for years I never knew any of my relatives in Connecticut.

My dad was born in Ansonia in 1917. Dad's father, George Albany Williams, was born in 1864 in Virginia. According to family records, he was born into slavery. Later, he married a woman named Mary Morgan. In the pictures that I've seen of the couple, Grandma Mary looks more European than black. But on my dad's birth certificate, it lists the race of both of my paternal grandparents as "Negro." I asked my dad about that one day, and he told me that back then it was illegal for a black person to marry a white person. African American history talks a lot about blacks who, for various reasons, attempted to "pass" for white. Rarer are stories about those people of European descent who decided to self-identify as black.

Passing was not an option for my mom in the late 1950s. New to the United States, and still fragile from the dysfunction of her early life, Mom experienced both a culture and marital shock that would send her to the state mental institution in Topeka more than once. In Korea, she had endured a hard childhood, with her parents dying young during the days of the Japanese occupation of Korea. After their death, Momma lived with an aunt and uncle who were mean to her. To survive, she dropped out of school as a third-grader and was forced to hustle and steal for food. As a result, she placed a high premium on feeding her children until we were full, even if it meant giving one of us her own portions. "Eat, eat," she'd urge us, in her sweet accent. I remember her trying to cook a stew-like dish for us one day, even while she was suffering one of her nervous breakdowns. She fought through the trembling and tears to finish cooking the meal. Even in her pain, she was determined to take care of us.

Surviving in Junk City

Dad later moved us to a hundred-year-old former railroad-worker house on the east side of Junction City near a grain elevator. He began his career as a garbage collector and was a hard, devoted worker until he was laid off two years before retirement.

I remember as a preschooler being taken on a tour of that old railroad house before we bought it. Years later, as an adult in 1989, I recall touring the house again before selling it for my dad for a paltry $3,000, which was all it was worth.

This house was also shaped like a box, with four rooms on the first floor and two rooms on the second. Back in the day, Momma put a "pee can" upstairs on the splintery wood floor so that whoever slept on that high second level didn't have to travel down the creaky steps in the middle of the night to use the bathroom. We had one "good" heater downstairs that Dad would only light before he left for work during the early morning, to help break the chill. My brother, George, and I slept in the same twin-size bed, under thick, homemade blankets. In the fall and winter, we would awake in the morning to see frost on our breath. In the summer, we had one window-unit air conditioner that cooled our drafty house more by the twirl of its fan than by the Freon inside of it.

During the night, I was afraid to go down to the living room where Momma often slept, because I knew that black, half-inch-long water bugs would be climbing the drapes and scurrying on the floor. Whenever I saw them, goose pimples rose on my body, and I could not resist the urge to squash as many of them as I could. Unfortunately, killing them also meant cleaning their slimy guts off the wood floor.

Living in Junction City wasn't like living in a typical Kansas town. (It didn't come by the nickname "Junk City" for nothing.) The town of 17,000 had a high concentration of crime, drugs, and prostitution that was no doubt spurred on by its proximity to Fort Riley.

Junction City's Ninth Street was so infamous that it became the title of a 1999 movie about Junction City, starring Martin Sheen and Isaac Hayes. The film, set in 1968, documented the deterioration of a community that was once celebrated for its rich history of African American music in the 1940s. By the Vietnam era, however, it had become "Junk City," a town now distinguished by blighted streets where strip clubs and juke joints replaced theaters and jazz clubs. Before long, the town tore down its disreputable elements and moved them to another main drag named Washington Street.

I remember seeing suspicious drug dealers in the row of one-room apartments across the street from our house. Next door to us my best friend, Gordon, along with his two brothers and sister, spent time in boys' homes or jail while their other sister, Melinda, stayed on the straight and narrow. One of our other neighbors, Clifford, who preferred to be called DeeDee, would go out on Washington Street on military paydays dressed as a woman to make a living as a prostitute.

A Normal Life?

All the while, my mother and father's marriage was plagued by strife. Mom complained of hearing voices, especially that of her mother who supposedly was a fortuneteller. Mom swore that the woman had placed a curse upon her when she was a little girl. Mom, who both spoke and yelled in broken English, also accused Dad of sitting with another woman at the downtown movie theater. With routine unpredictability, she'd fly into jealous fits that only silence and the passage of hours would calm.

Dad, whose years in the military had taught him to endure tons of stress without complaint, rode out the storms of marital turmoil with a steely demeanor that many probably mistook for indifference. In fact, he quietly hungered for brighter days. He was by no means a perfect husband or father, but he did seem to desire a better life for his family. Unfortunately, that "better life" always seemed to elude us. Mom desperately wanted to be loved by her husband in her new land, but mental unrest routinely overpowered her sense of peace.

My brothers and sisters and I just wanted to live a normal, American life—even if we had no idea what that really looked like. We just knew we wanted to escape the box.

In *Anna Karenina,* Tolstoy famously wrote, "Happy families are all alike, but every unhappy family is unhappy in its own way."

I think that was the Russian novelist's way of saying there are no perfect families. We all have issues and baggage that make us as unique as snowflakes. My family had a blizzard's worth. Yet, even in our dysfunction, our poverty, and our pain, there can be happiness. It may not look like the middle-America-everybody-smile-for-the-camera variety of happiness, but it was happiness nonetheless.

God has a way, I would soon discover, of pulling sunshine out of the bleakest of skies.

CHAPTER 2

"Danger, Andrew Williams!"
(Or, How I Caught the Computer Science Bug)

My interest in science and technology was stirring inside, even as I was roaming wheat fields and shooting BB guns. As a kid, I remember seeing reruns of classic shows like *Lost in Space*, *Star Trek*, and *The Jetsons* and thinking, *I want to live in that world*.

There aren't many pictures of me as a child (I chalk it up to the "sixth child syndrome"), but I do remember one telling photo of me as a nine-year-old. In it I'm wearing a bent-up clothes hanger on my head as if it were some kind of 1950s Martian helmet.

Our parents couldn't afford a lot of toys, but the ones we did have spurred my imagination like crazy. In retrospect, *not* having that many toys to play with as a young child probably spurred my imagination even more. Since Dad worked part of his career as a garbage collector, occasionally he would find used toys and bring them home to us. I remember trying to build "spaceships" with various types of blocks and bricks, since we didn't have Legos back then.

Invasion of the Robots

I watched every rerun episode of *Lost in Space* on our old black-and-white TV. The campy show from the '60s was about the Robinson family's brave mission to colonize a distant planet. But when a foreign spy (the devious Dr. Smith!) sneaks aboard the spaceship before its launch to sabotage it, he winds up trapped aboard the craft himself. His extra weight knocks the ship off course and the Robinsons and their crew become—"lost in space." Essentially, the show was a space-age retelling of *The Swiss Family Robinson*.

Robot B-9, who was part of the Robinson family's crew, always intrigued me. He represented my first taste of a robot that was truly autonomous, one that could think, reason, and communicate on its own. He had sensors to detect trouble and often warned the show's young protagonist with the famous warning, "Danger, Will Robinson!" He had motors that moved his arms and propelled the wheels and joints on his "legs." His power came from a battery back that could be removed. At times, he would even show emotion.

The depiction of robots in media and pop culture has evolved over the years. In 1956, years before *Lost in Space,* there was Robby the Robot, the towering mechanical creature from the cult-classic film *The Forbidden Planet.* In 1968, a few years after the premiere of *Lost in Space,* the groundbreaking *2001: A Space Odyssey* arrived in movie theaters. With the brilliant but duplicitous HAL 9000, the film set the science-fiction archetype for the notion of artificial intelligence in a robot. Nine years later, the *Odd Couple*-like tandem of R2-D2 and C-3PO helped turn *Star Wars* into a cultural phenomenon. Then, ten years after that came the progressively humanized android Data in *Star Trek: The Next Generation,* a follow-up to the iconic '60s television show and its movies. In 2008, Disney and Pixar presented yet another robot with human-like yearnings in the animated hit, *WALL-E.* Throughout all of these portrayals, there seems to be one common thread: Mechanical beings who, through their interactions with humans, become less robotic and more human themselves. In many instances, their "humanity" also served as a sort of contrasting point to the frequent in-humanity of the humans around them.

Child of Invention

As a kid, I used to sit around and dream up inventions all day long. During one particularly inspired moment, I used the back of a napkin to draw a design for a model rocket that would first be lifted into the air with the help of a balloon and then be powered by an engine that would ignite after a timed fuse went off. The top of the rocket had a pin that would burst the balloon after the timed ignition of the engine. (It was a possible forerunner to the space shuttle, with its combination of an external fuel tank and reusable boosters.) On rainy days, my friends and I constructed elaborate little boats from sticks. We'd watch them float down the flooded curb to the end of our street, where they deposited into a huge puddle. In our minds, it was like the great Mississippi emptying boats into the Atlantic Ocean.

My regular visits to the library found me hunting for books that would give me ideas for designs and inventions. On one occasion I found a book that gave instructions for making a rain detector. My version had a battery-powered circuit and bell whose connection would be completed if the contacts (made with a clothespin) were brought together by the gradual disappearance of Alka-Seltzer tablets, which would dissolve after they got wet from the rain. Yep, I was destined to be a scientist.

Junction City Public Education

Although we were considered low-income, I received a great education from the public high schools in Junction City. Washington Elementary was located just a couple blocks from our house on 15th and Washington streets. I can't remember having a bad teacher throughout my education in Junction City.

During the summer prior to kindergarten, I was so nervous

about not being able to tie my shoes in time for the school year that my dad spent extra time out on our creaky front porch trying to teach me. Eventually, I got it.

In kindergarten, I enjoyed watching *Sesame Street* as part of our curriculum, playing with educational toys, learning the alphabet and numbers, taking naps, and drawing and coloring pictures. My teacher was Mrs. Zimbado, a gray-haired white woman who was nice most of the time.

I say "most of the time" because there was one unpleasant moment etched into my memory. One day during art time, I tried to draw a picture of our "mixed" dog, Chubby. Chubby, who was a blend of Spitz and some other unknown breed, had a snow-white coat. Unfortunately, I didn't have a white crayon at my disposal. So, I used yellow.

When Mrs. Zimbado saw my picture, she seemed troubled. "Is your dog yellow?" she asked.

"No, ma'am. He's white."

She became upset with me and suddenly grabbed my hand, with the crayon still in it, and started to guide my hand to mark out my yellow Chubby.

I was so shaken by this that I wanted to cry, but I somehow held it together. Why would she be so upset over my yellow Chubby? Was this another instance of someone trying to put me in a box?

My ten-year-old brother, Morgan, met me at lunchtime to walk me home from my half-day kindergarten class. By this time, I was sobbing and he couldn't understand what I was trying to tell him.

In general, it helped that my five siblings were good in school. By the time I reached a higher grade, my teachers would brag about Mary or Jeanne or Robert being a good student. My buddies from the East Side didn't have the same fortune. Their siblings were known either for sports, delinquency, or both.

I saw firsthand how low expectations shaped the way certain teachers would talk to some of my African American buddies— and how higher expectations, because of my siblings, may have helped me win some favor. More importantly, I wanted to do well in school because my parents and siblings expected it.

"I believe Andrew may-ka [i.e., make] all As," Momma would smile and say as she hugged me.

"You have a better chance if you get a good education than if you try to become a pro athlete," Dad would chime in. "Some people are bigger, stronger, and faster than you are and practice a lot more hours. You should be well-rounded like Paul Robeson."

We didn't have a lot of money for toys, but I quickly learned that Dad would cough up cash for anything related to education. In third grade I needed the sixteen-count box of crayons. I lied and told him I needed the sixty-four-count crayon box, with the built-in sharpener, and he bought it for me!

Even then, I was learning how to use education to my advantage.

CHAPTER 3

Little Church
Near the Prairie

We were not what you'd call a churchgoing family. Dad had attended the local Baptist church as a little boy, but so did everyone from his generation. While he didn't reject the notion of God, it clearly was not at the forefront of his mind as an adult. Mom grew up as a Buddhist, but she, too, had drifted away from whatever religious traditions she had kept as a child.

Consequently, we were not atheist, agnostic, or antichurch; we were nothing. Like many Americans back then and today, we existed in that dispassionate realm of simply not knowing any better.

That is why we were all taken aback when my oldest brother, Robert, got out of bed early one Sunday morning and announced, "I'm going to look for a church today."

The Young Seeker

Actually, we shouldn't have been that surprised. Robert, who was fourteen at the time, was always the most curious about what went on inside churches. *What were all those people doing in there every week?* he'd wonder. Despite my family's general indifference, he had developed an interest in religion and what happens to people after they die.

Robert came to his Sunday-morning declaration after finding a Bible tract that someone had left on a park bench on the corner of Sixth and Washington streets. The little pamphlet talked about heaven and hell and God's love. It ended with a brief presentation of the plan of salvation and an invitation to pray and "accept Jesus Christ as your Lord and Savior."

Robert told me later that he didn't understand everything that the tract said when he read it that day. "I had no idea what it meant from a theological perspective," he said. "But I guess my heart was ready, and I prayed the prayer. For me, that Bible tract left on that park bench by a stranger changed my life."

After praying to receive Jesus into his heart, Robert began feeling uneasy about staying at home on Sunday morning. "Something inside told me that I needed to be in church," he recalls.

So Robert decided to visit Junction City Free Methodist, the little brick church on Thirteenth Street, two blocks over from our house. It was the church he often passed when he rode his bicycle around the neighborhood.

The walk to the church was nerve-racking for Robert. All the way there, his heart thumped like a college step team in competition. When Robert reached his destination, he saw a white man with slick, silver hair standing on the sidewalk outside the church. "May I help you, young man?" he asked. He could tell Robert was nervous.

"I'm looking for a church," Robert said timidly.

"Well, you've found one right here," the man said. "You're welcome to come in."

Suddenly, sweat started to soak through Robert's shirt. He wondered, *Will these white people really welcome a Korean American kid from a mixed family into their church?* Then he panicked. Without thinking, he told the man he was looking for the Baptist church, even though he knew the Baptist church was across the street from our grade school.

The man smiled and gave him the directions. Robert turned and started to walk away. But then something happened.

"I walked across the street," Robert recalls, "and it felt like an altar call because I hesitated, argued with myself, and finally surrendered, turned around, and headed back to the Free Methodist Church."

The white man was still standing there, waiting and smiling knowingly. Without saying a word, he put his arms around Robert's shoulders and walked him into the church.

"My life was never the same from that day forward," Robert says today. In fact, none of our lives were.

Winning a Family for Christ

The white man's name was Warren Martin. He was the Sunday school superintendent of the church whose family had been a part of the congregation from its earliest days. The congregation itself had a fluctuating, transient membership of twenty-five to seventy-five people because of the military families that would attend, and most of them were white.

In the weeks that followed, the leaders from JC Free Methodist not only poured themselves into discipling Robert, but they came after all of the Williams children.

Several people from JC Free Methodist would come to our house, asking my parents for permission to take all six of us to church. Mr. Martin's mother-in-law, Merle Fawley, was the church's oldest matriarch. She made it her personal mission to get all of us to Sunday school. But my dad was not so keen on the idea. Frankly, he was distrustful of what those white people would be teaching us.

But Mrs. Fawley was not deterred. She would stand on our front porch, with the storm door between her and Dad. "Mr. Williams, we'd like for your children to attend our Sunday school," she'd say.

Dad would wave his hand and say, "No," then turn away and have one of us close the door. One day, after weeks of unsuccessful visits, Mrs. Fawley stealthily maneuvered her way into the house as Dad turned to walk back into the living room—she opened the storm door, walked in, and grabbed Dad's hand. She said, "Mr. Williams, if you allow your children to come to our church, I give you my word we will take care of them."

Dad, impressed by the woman's moxie, laughed and said, "Okay, okay." Mrs. Fawley thanked him, and that was the beginning of our life in Sunday school, and our chance to finally get the full story on Jesus and why He was so important.

Though Dad and Mom did not attend JC Free Methodist with us, from then on they were fully supportive of the idea. In fact, on those Sundays when Mom was stricken by her mental illness and unable to function, Dad even made sure our shoes were shined and that we each had a quarter for the offering plate.

A Bond Beyond Sunday School

Mr. Martin's daughter, Sharon Scoggins, was my first Sunday School teacher at JC Free Methodist. I was a bouncy three-year-old, still in diapers, when I arrived in her nursery class—at least that's what I'm told. (I'd like to think I had it together enough to be out of diapers by then, but oh well . . .)

Mrs. Scoggins came from a long line of Free Methodists. Her dad had literally helped build the small stone church on Thirteenth Street in the mid-1940s. Her grandmother, Mrs. Fawley, had been a spiritual leader in her family since before those early days of JC Free Methodist. Grandma Fawley's passion for witnessing and teaching people about the love of Jesus was infectious. That same passion was evident in her granddaughter, too.

When I talked to Mrs. Scoggins years later, she informed me that I was a precocious student. Apparently, I responded well to a Sunday school curriculum that repeated the Bible story four consecutive weeks from slightly different angles. According to my former teacher, I was especially good at picking up on the Bible memory verses.

She particularly remembered the lessons she taught me about Moses—how as a baby he was put into a basket and protected by God. Mrs. Scoggins thought that story was a beautiful picture of what God eventually did for my family. Maybe, she told me, the cardboard box I slept in as a baby was a symbol of God's protection and provision in my life.

Mrs. Scoggins was also privy to my mom's struggles, how she would lapse into sudden nervous breakdowns. During the seasons of Momma's emotional distress, my dad often would become sleep deprived and need a break from watching Momma. Mrs. Scoggins and her husband, David, were living in the basement of her father's house, and she recalled that sometimes her father would bring my mom to his home in order to give my dad a break.

Mrs. Scoggins knew that Momma's illness was rooted in the hardship of her childhood and the ordeal of living through the war in her country. Mrs. Scoggins and her family understood that Momma was not "crazy" but sick, and they were there to pray and support my family through many of our darkest times.

Sharon and Dave Scoggins celebrated their first Christmas as a married couple in 1967, that same year that Mrs. Scoggins became my Sunday school teacher. Though I was young, I vividly remember the two of them bringing my family food and gifts on Christmas Eve. That was the Christmas that I received my beloved blue shirt with the red trim; it was the only present that I received that year.

Mrs. Scoggins used to say if anything ever happened to our mom and dad, she wanted to adopt us. And she was serious. After a while, my sisters Jeanne and Mary began calling Mrs. Scoggins their second "mom," which moved her profoundly.

My family's bond with the folks from JC Free Methodist was a deep and meaningful one that helped shape us into the people we are today. No matter what type of churches my siblings and I attend today (I later would become a Baptist), we will always have a little bit of Free Methodist planted firmly inside us.

CHAPTER 4

Tales of a
Fifth-Grade Elijah

I eventually learned that the Free Methodist denomination is an offshoot of Wesleyan, Nazarene, and other Holiness church traditions. The Free Methodist founders were committed abolitionists who supported freedom for all slaves in the United States. It was founded in 1860, a year before the start of the American Civil War.

The "Free" was derived from the group's abolitionist roots, as well as the fact that the founders opposed the practice of charging worshipers a fee for sanctuary seats that were closer to the pulpit, which had apparently become common in some churches during that period.

The Christians at JC Free Methodist were exceedingly conservative in their theology and beliefs about social activities like dancing, gambling, and imbibing. They even frowned upon women wearing jewelry. But, unlike many fundamentalist Christians in those days, this didn't mean they abstained from civic involvement. In fact, Mr. Martin actually ran for state political office one year on the Prohibitionist Party ticket. (To the relief of all the bar owners in Junk City, he didn't win.)

Pastor Bill Howard, a tall, bespectacled man with a booming voice that seemed custom-made for preaching, was the shepherd of the flock. He and his wife, Lily, were there during my first few years at JC. Along with Grandma Fawley and Mrs. Scoggins, Mrs. Howard was one of the church's main Sunday school teachers.

As a child, I had the gospel drilled into my heart and mind, week after week. By the time I was nine, in 1973, I had come forward for the altar call at least a half-dozen times. I knew who Jesus was and what He had done for me—that He bled and died to save my soul. But I also began to feel all the guilt that came with an awareness of my sinfulness. It became harder to tell my parents a lie or sneak a piece of candy before dinner. In adult terms, my salvation wasn't just a concept; it had taken root in my heart.

I loved memorizing Bible verses and singing the kids' praise songs of our day—"Jesus Loves Me," "Deep and Wide," "He's Got the Whole World in His Hands." Every Sunday morning was as fun as Saturday-morning cartoons. I was a passionate, pint-sized follower of Jesus.

Pursuing Perfection

When I turned ten, I experienced a spiritual turning point. As I said, our church was very conservative. The preachers and teachers often talked about something called "entire sanctification." In layman terms, they believed that through holy and obedient living you could gradually reach a point where you were totally free of sin. Some folks called it Christian Perfection and often spoke of "going on to perfection."

Once a year, a Native American family called the Weesaws would come and do a revival service at the church. Delmar Weesaw was a fiery evangelist who cried when he preached. His oldest daughter, Delmona, played the accordion and was a wonderful singer. Louise, the middle child, accompanied her sister on vocals.

The youngest sister, Lydia, played the drums. Mrs. Weesaw, who had long dark hair, usually ministered to the women who would come forward.

Mr. Weesaw commanded an audience's attention. In between the shouting and crying, he would talk about the old Holiness way and how Christians should be on the journey to being entirely sanctified. Looking back now, I realize that the message was perhaps a bit too extreme. Were they telling us that being saved wasn't enough? But as a kid, I was frightened into believing that I needed to be "going on to perfection."

The flip side of this doctrine was that they believed you could lose your salvation, a pretty scary proposition for a little boy. Can you imagine the anxiety of punching your sister or lying about your homework and then wondering whether you were "in" or "out" of heaven? I was especially worried during the scary summer nights when the tornado sirens would go off. Kansas has always been known for its busy tornado season, so the local emergency alert siren went off as commonly as the police sirens on Ninth and Washington streets. Our Fifteenth Street house didn't have a basement, so I was afraid that it would be swept away like Dorothy's. One good funnel cloud, and our flimsy little box would be on its way to Oz. So on stormy nights, I would rush to "ask Jesus into my heart" once again, just to make sure I could squeak by and get into heaven should that be my last day on Earth.

Still, I was usually determined to be a good Christian, and not just because of the threat of tornadoes. I loved Jesus and my heart was very sensitive towards God. I wanted to do things for Him.

I remember going up to the altar after Mr. Weesaw gave an invitation and just wanting to be entirely sanctified, just wanting the Lord to have complete control in my life. A lot of what the leaders talked about was external, like men wearing long-sleeved shirts and women wearing dresses. And so, I would go up to the altar in tears, crying and praying and pleading with God to make me clean. After that, I carried my Bible to school and prayed constantly.

After one particularly convicting Sunday sermon, I was filled with the urge to tell more people about Jesus. I thought to myself, *I need to be a witness.* So I would go door-to-door in the neighborhood and try to share the gospel, telling people, "Jesus loves you." Some folks smiled, others wondered what this crazy kid was doing on their porch. On some Sundays, the church would have a testimony time; and even though I was a fifth-grader, I was one of the first to share what God was doing in my life.

Pride and Imperfection

After a while Mr. Hinebaugh, who was Robert's Sunday school teacher, started calling me Elijah. Elijah, of course, was the prophet who raised the dead, confronted the priests of Baal, brought fire down from the sky, and ascended to heaven in a chariot. At age ten I didn't have that much Holy Ghost power, but I was pretty pleased to have the nickname.

Soon, my spiritual sincerity began to morph into something that smelled more like spiritual pride. When the Howards accepted a call to another church, a new pastor came to JC Free Methodist. Pastor Terry was a younger man, fresh out of seminary. Seeing my spiritual precociousness, he offered to have a special Bible study with me. "Andrew," he said, "I'd love to help you grow in your faith." But I was insulted. I thought I knew more than he did about the Bible.

One Sunday morning during the sermon, I thought to myself, *God wants me to stand up and give a testimony.* This wouldn't have been too unusual with Reverend Howard, but Pastor Terry rebuked me and told me to sit down. This rankled some of the older church members, who felt that the preacher wasn't allowing the Holy Spirit to dictate the service. But to tell the truth, I really thought what I had to say was more insightful than what that pastor was telling us. For a fifth-grader, I had become pretty full of myself.

But I didn't see that then. More than anything, I was confused. If God didn't allow me to speak, I thought, I must have not been living a sinless enough life.

Around this time, our church went to the Junction City Municipal Auditorium to see a charismatic preacher named Ron McFadden. Our church wasn't charismatic at all, so it was the first time many of us had seen someone who was charismatic.

Somehow, not surprisingly, I ended up in the thick of things. During part of the service, the preacher delivered prophecies to different people from the audience, which numbered about three hundred. I don't recall how I ended up on his radar, but he called me to the stage and gave me a prophecy.

"Andrew," he said (I had told him my name), "God is going to use you in a great way . . ."

This, of course, didn't help my spiritual pride one bit. But it did boost my burgeoning sense of purpose.

CHAPTER 5

Losing My Religion

In sixth grade, my well-intentioned but immature zeal led me into a few sticky situations. I was very sincere in doing what I thought was pleasing to God, but I didn't always consider the practical implications of my passion. One day, for reasons I can no longer recall, I wanted to kneel down and pray during class. My teacher, Mrs. Rosa, wouldn't let me. "I'm sorry, Andrew, that wouldn't be appropriate," she said.

I felt like I was being persecuted for my faith. I was still carrying my Bible to school and silently praying at lunchtime and before tests. But, in my pursuit of entire sanctification, I wanted to ramp up my spiritual commitment even more. Modeling godly prayer for my teacher and classmates—and thus demonstrating my commendable piety—was just one way to get some extra notches on my sanctification belt.

"Andrew, it's okay to be enthusiastic about your religious beliefs," Mrs. Rosa explained to me, "but you have to respect other people, too."

I do respect them, I remember thinking. *But that's why I'm doing what God wants me to do.* Had I only listened more closely in church, I would have learned that God wanted me to listen to my teachers and respect authority instead of living based on my artificial rules and guidelines.

When I got to seventh grade, I still carried my Bible and prayed. I was still a good student, too, making straight As. But I was growing less certain of the effectiveness of my devotion.

I read my Bible. I prayed. I told people about Jesus. So why wasn't I living a completely sinless life? Why wasn't I even close? I don't remember telling fibs, having nasty thoughts, or saying cruel things to my siblings. But I remember thinking of all the good things I still wasn't doing and not measuring up. I felt like I couldn't do enough to make God love me more and cancel out my sin. Arrogant pride was my biggest problem. Why wasn't my complete sanctification kicking in?

Then peer pressure gripped me. Wanting to be liked by all the new kids from the other elementary schools, especially that cute girl on the track team who wrote me notes, started mattering more to me than the opinions of my parents, people from church, or God. When I impressed other kids, I received immediate social gratification—the instant reward of being "cool." The payoff wasn't as swift on the spiritual front.

Science had taught me that good experiments are observable, repeatable, and able to predict new facts and events. I had given the "Christian perfection" theory all I could, but the results were wanting. Perhaps it was a bad experiment. Perhaps it was time to focus my attention on other things. I was, after all, finally a teenager.

I recalled hearing a song with the chorus, "If Jesus isn't Lord of all, then He's not Lord at all." Though the songwriter was clearly trying to motivate listeners to restore Jesus to His rightful place in their lives, I focused on the chorus's converse implication. I had made Jesus Lord of all, and where had it gotten me? *Well,* I reasoned, *if I can't live a sinless life, then I'm probably not a Christian.* It was my way of excusing myself from the guilt and shame of putting my once-passionate faith on the back burner.

My reasoning went something like this:
God hates sin, so He hates me unless I get Jesus back into my heart. And because Jesus is God, Jesus hates sin too. Therefore, if I have sin in me, He can't be in me.

The Cool Crowd

By junior high school—seventh through ninth grade—my interest in science (and science fiction) had blossomed, but so had my interest in sports. Prior to starting junior high school, I won the position of quarterback on my school's football team. In one hard-fought game against our archrivals from nearby Westwood Elementary, we tried to run a play that involved sneaking the quarterback into the end zone for a touchdown, but we kept getting called for penalties. I remember the euphoria when I was finally able to scuttle in and score.

I also loved playing basketball. And my buddies and I played a lot—at school, at the local playground, you name it. Sometimes I would take a bus across the Republican River to Fort Riley, where I would play with the soldiers on base. I was like a shrub in a forest of oak trees, but playing with older guys made me a better player. However, it also exposed me to the kind of "mature" stuff that older guys jive about as they're playing ball—and particularly older guys who are in the Army. My homeys from the East Side could cuss up a storm too—even as elementary school kids. But it was fun to hang out with men.

During the summer between seventh and eighth grades, I started sneaking off to some of the weekend parties for the "cool" crowd. There was dancing, which was especially scandalous since the Free Methodist Church forbade such activities for its members. My rebellion was on.

Even in middle school, friends of mine like Derek Johnson and Gene Bailey (the names are changed to protect the guilty) were already smoking cigarettes and experimenting with marijuana. My initiation began one day at a neighbor's house. In the back alley I saw a cigarette butt. I picked it up and used my friend's matches to light it.

That was the first time I smoked. I remember that first smoke felt a lot cooler in my mouth and throat than I thought it would. There was something surprisingly sweet about tasting the forbidden fruit. It was probably inevitable that I would experiment with cigarettes. My mom was an accomplished chain-smoker. Her biggest obstacle to the Christian faith was being told that a person couldn't smoke and still be a Christian. My dad had been a chain-smoker as well, until a doctor informed him if he didn't quit he was going to die soon. Booze was my dad's vice of choice, but he managed to keep it hidden from us until one day when I was in grade school my brother Morgan found his stash and confronted him with this: "Dad, if you drink I'm going to drink, too." Feeling exposed and convicted, my dad poured out his entire supply of booze. He didn't drink again after that.

At a few of those weekend parties, I remember drinking beer for the first time—and not enjoying it. I figured beer drinking must be an acquired taste. The only beer I came close to liking was Schlitz Malt Liquor. Derek and Gene offered me a marijuana cigarette. "Come on, man, try it," they said. They teased me, saying that I was a church boy and wouldn't do it.

I recall feeling a twinge of trepidation, but it wasn't enough to lead me to resist the invitation. I smoked the joint. Beyond the basic curiosity, I also wanted to show them and others that "Yeah, I don't go to church anymore."

What started as casual took on a more serious complexion as I spent more time in this new rebellious culture. I remembered going with Derek and Gene to a drug dealer's house where we bought and smoked more mari-juana. I probably smoked marijuana five times altogether, but each of those occasions no doubt stripped away a part of my soul. I felt myself becoming less like me and increasingly empty inside.

Higher and Higher

My mom and dad could see that I was no longer the passionate Christian that I had once been, but they didn't suspect the depths of my moral descent. My church family, I think, knew something sinister was awry, but I did my best to avoid sustained contact with them. Sunday mornings were still my favorite time of the week, but not for religious reasons any longer. They were now my best mornings for sleeping in. I used to love going disco roller skating on Friday and Saturday nights. My brother George had gotten me hooked on skating parties. George used to go with his friends to skating parties as far away as Kansas City. Later, Fort Riley converted one of its basketball gyms into a roller skating rink for the soldiers, women, and high schoolers to go to on the weekends, and I was out there on the middle of the floor trying to show off my moves. Believe it or not, my dad, in his 50s, was the one who first taught me to skate backwards. I used to skate all the way down to the Seventeenth Street park in order to practice my moves—and hang with my boys.

Just when I was starting to believe I could maintain my new carefree life, my brother Robert wanted to talk to me.

"Andrew, I saw you at that park yesterday," he said.

Uh-oh. What did he know? Was my cover at risk of being blown?

"So what?" I said, putting up a tough front. "I'm at the playground all the time."

"I think I saw you smoking and drinking," he continued. "You better be careful what you get involved in, because you may regret it later."

"You can follow me around all you want, but you won't find anything," I thought to myself, knowing within that my secret life of rebellion was in jeopardy. I had to watch my back.

It didn't take long, however, for me to mess up—drugs tend to have that effect.

I was out one night playing basketball with my friends on the west side of town. I should tell you, playing basketball on drugs was a rather bizarre experience. On the court, I had the invincible feeling that I could run faster and jump higher than anyone else.

Suddenly, my brothers Morgan and George drove up.

"Ah, man," I remember saying to the guys, "it's my brothers."

"Come on, let's go home," Morgan said, as he got out of the car.

"We're just hanging out, playing some hoops."

But Morgan knew better. He could tell immediately that I was high. After a brief but no less embarrassing exchange, he hustled me into the car to take me home.

That was the first—and last—time I remember being high around a family member. I had a glazed-over look, and everything I said was punctuated by nervous laughter. I sat in the backseat of the car feeling embarrassed and guilty. I wasn't sure where my life was heading.

Out of the Abyss

Up until eighth grade, I received nothing less than an A in my courses. I was exceptionally conscientious with my schoolwork. Besides being fascinated by the wonder of science and the adventure of discovering new things, from a young age I wanted to prove that African Americans were just as good as everyone else, just as my dad had always impressed upon me.

I remember whenever there was a black NFL quarterback or coach, Dad would be so proud and brag all about it to me. I longed for him to be proud of me and brag about me. He never would while I was growing up. I always sought his approval, but he never said he was proud of my accomplishments or that he loved me. Funny how one day I would realize that he did love me, but he just was expressing it the only way he knew how—going to work and providing food and clothes for me. So seeking his approval was one of the reasons I would study harder and ask God to help me in everything I did. Unfortunately, I laid aside those good habits during my rebellion period, and eventually I saw the damage it was inflicting on my success as a student.

During my freshman year in high school, I got my first B. Later on, while taking my eleventh-grade Algebra II and Trigonometry class, I got a D. What was going on?

For a long time, I had been able to pull those As while going to parties and having a good time. Now I was slipping. This got my attention.

At the same time, I was vying for a spot on the school basketball team. At five foot five, I was still on the short side compared to the other boys. I had heard that cigarettes and drugs like marijuana could possibly stunt a young person's growth. Was I sabotaging any chance I had of reaching Dr. J's height? My mom was only four foot eight, and I was scared I wouldn't grow to be much taller.

The prospect of poor grades, no sports, and my parents finding me out were enough to rescue me from my cold indifference. I wanted good grades, and I wanted to be a superior athlete who could play above the rim, and I didn't want to disappoint Momma and Dad. So that was it. I quit messing with drugs for good.

Slowly, I began pulling myself up from the abyss and back to respectability as a student and athlete. I made the basketball team. And though I didn't start, I was often the first player off the bench. I was achieving success and having fun.

But I was still spiritually empty. And the God-shaped hole I was carrying around inside seemed wider than ever.

What Price Glory?

When you've fallen away from God after being so single-mindedly devoted to Him at a young age, regaining your focus can be a difficult thing. I was lost and knew it. How had I fallen so far? I wanted to get back the excitement and joy that I once felt for God. But I also wanted to embrace the freedom and daring to be the teenager that I was. High school life was full of fun and possibility, both academically and socially. I wanted to take advantage of it—and I tried my hardest.

Still, all along the way I knew I would never be truly fulfilled until I got back into rhythm with God.

I went on a rapid growth spurt between my sophomore and junior years that swung open new doors. My five-foot-five frame shot up to almost six feet, and I took full advantage of it on the basketball court. My jump shot and defense improved markedly. And on a really good day, I could even dunk the ball. As a high school athlete, these were my glory days.

During my junior year, I started getting letters of interest from colleges that wanted me for their academic programs. It was enough to swell a young guy's head, and I was no exception. The situation was not helped by an unforgettable moment from my senior year, when my team, the Junction City Blue Jays, played our archrivals, the Indians, from nearby Manhattan (Kansas) High.

The game had all the makings of a blowout. We were losing badly in the third quarter. A lack of hustle and a lackadaisical defense had put us in a deep hole. Though I started games occasionally, my primary role had been to provide a scoring punch off the bench. So when Coach Beck looked down the bench and called my name, I was given the chance to live one of those dream moments. I took a deep breath, swallowed hard, and played like my personal safety depended on it. Thankfully, my shooting stroke was in effect that night, and I scored thirteen points in ten minutes. We won the game, and I was the hero of the hour. After that I wanted to be known as "Instant Offense."

My friends from gym class made a cheer for me that the home crowd chanted whenever I came off the bench. They would clap their hands and stomp their feet in rhythm, *"What's that word when you're bustin' loose, say Drew-say, Drew-say – Drew-say, Drew-say!"* (Drew was my basketball nickname.) Students and adults from throughout the community screamed it at the top of their lungs.

Later, the local newspaper featured an article about my success as the team's most valuable player off the bench. Mimicking the old Rolaids ad, the headline read: "How Does JCHS spell relief? A-N-D-R-E-W W-I-L-L-I-A-M-S." In the article, I'm quoted talking about how I wanted to become an electrical engineer, because my brother Robert, who had gone to college while in the Air Force, had become an electrical engineer. So I knew engineers made good salaries. But I would need to strike a better balance between my athletic pursuits and my academic interests if I expected to ever get into college.

Missed Opportunities

It probably didn't help that I was also dating a sophomore. Lisa Benson (not her real name) was my first genuine girlfriend, and I thought I was in love. My dad never gave me "the talk," so I was clueless about matters of sex and intimate relationships. I still had enough Bible teaching in my head to know that sex outside of marriage was not right, but that didn't keep me from yearning for the same kind of carnal bliss that many of my peers were enjoying.

The night I took Lisa to the spring dance, my plan was to drive her to a special spot near the river and see what happened. I was anxious for an opportunity to, you know, demonstrate my fondness for her. Much to my hidden chagrin, however, we ended up hanging out with some other friends.

Before I knew it, my opportunity had faded. I look back now and realize it must've been God protecting me, because the flesh certainly was willing. (But more on that later.)

The recurring incidence of situations like that, I now understand, was proof that God was not as far away from me as I thought. He had not given up on me.

CHAPTER 6

Higher Learning

The good news is that I got out of high school alive. The old hymn says, "Through many dangers, toils, and snares I have already come." Every time I sing that song, I remember my teenage years and the many reasons why I shouldn't be where I am today. And yet, Amazing Grace saw fit to spare me from the disaster my life should've been, between the drugs, pride, and indifference that once ensnared me.

One sure sign of God's mercy is that, despite my rebellion, I managed to stay engaged enough in school to graduate and go on to college. In addition to not wanting to disappoint my parents, I credit that achievement to Asteroids, Space Invaders, Star Raiders, and almost any other sci-fi video game that you could find at the local arcade in the late seventies and early eighties.

Allow me to explain.

The first time I ever used a computer was in 1977 in junior high school, when I visited my brother Morgan at the University of Kansas (or KU) for a weekend. He was majoring in aerospace engineering, and I was ecstatic to receive an inside peek at KU's engineering department.

As Morgan worked on a project in the lab, he let me play a *Star Trek* game that was on the campus mainframe computer. The "computer" I played the game on back then had only a keyboard for inputting commands and a dot-matrix line printer to output the game status. Whenever I wanted to move from one space quadrant to another, I would select the coordinates and then wait for the printer to redraw what the "outer space" around me looked like—where the Klingon battle cruisers were, where the refueling stations were, and so on. There was a lot more left to the imagination than what exists in today's high-intensity, graphics-driven video games. Nevertheless, I was fascinated and intrigued. The experience left me determined to learn how to build computers and video games.

That same weekend, Morgan took my brother George and me to the video arcade. He had picked up ten dollars' worth of quarters from the bank in anticipation of our visit, and we played Asteroids all night. I was hooked on Asteroids.

When I got to high school, my interest in computers continued. Seeing my brother Robert become an electrical engineer kindled my interest in pursuing engineering myself. I probably wouldn't have known there was such a thing as an engineer had it not been for my brother becoming one.

One of the helpful things that came out of Dad being laid off two years before he was to retire was that he started collecting Social Security, and since I was his dependent I was eligible to receive some money as well. After a few months of saving, I was able to afford my very own personal computer. I decided to buy an Atari 400, because it came with the game Star Raiders—the granddaddy of all 3-D space games at that time.

In high school, students in the gifted program had access to a TRS-80 computer, a privilege that I took full advantage of. Later, the school got a computer lab with Apple IIe computers. Now, I was really in business.

Dad had convinced me that the odds were against me making it in professional basketball—"Andrew, there's about a million black teenagers who can shoot a ball just as good or better than you but won't make it into the NBA," he said. "But look at George Washington Carver. He invented three hundred ways to use the peanut." While I wasn't interested in inventing new forms of peanut butter, I understood his point. He wanted me to use my mind to advance science and my career, and not have to endure the hard labor he used to tell me about. One time I saw my dad dig a huge ditch in our backyard to find a leak in one of our pipes. He enjoyed it because it reminded him of the hard physical labor he had to endure during the Great Depression. I continued to play ball in high school, but I began viewing computers and engineering as my ticket to making money and being successful. I toyed with the idea of becoming a physician, but my lack of success in chemistry deterred me from that field. Engineering was calling my name.

Fatherly Advice

Dad never attended any of my graduations or sporting events, but he supported all of my educational endeavors. All six of us kids ended up going to college either by scholarships, loans, or financial aid.

Kansas's public university system served my family well, and Kansas State, in nearby Manhattan, was the primary choice for the majority of my siblings—my brother George majored in computer science at K-State; my sister Mary studied English there; my other sister, Jeannie, majored in art education and Spanish; and Robert, of course, majored in electrical engineering and eventually went on to get his Ph.D. there at University of Dayton. Morgan was the exception. He attended the University of Kansas in Lawrence, and then went on to earn two master's degrees from MIT.

I did well on my PSAT and ACT exams in high school, so I received recruitment letters from elite institutions like MIT, Harvard, and Stanford. My dad had never gone to college, so in his usual understated way he was very proud. He suggested I start at one of the state universities and then attend a school like MIT for my graduate degree, just as Morgan had done. I didn't want to go to K-State because it was too close to home, and too many of my siblings had gone there. K-State's extreme rural setting also put me off. In high school, the Manhattan students sometimes said racially derogatory things about our basketball team when we'd play there, since we had a lot of black players. I didn't want to live with that for four years.

But Morgan had good things to say about KU. As one of Junction City High's Kansas Merit Scholars, I had the opportunity to take a trip to KU for a tour. Marshall Jackson, an admissions director at KU, invited several minority high schools from all around Kansas for a weekend visit to the campus. One of the first things I noticed was the larger number of minority students there compared to K-State, which immediately put me at ease.

And then I met her. Kara Mills (not her real name) was a senior from Leavenworth High School and the reigning Miss Teen of Kansas. I was immediately captured by her charm and beauty, and I was happy to discover that she seemed to have a mutual interest. We exchanged phone numbers and decided we would stay in touch. And that did it for me. I developed an instant crush. If Kara Mills was going to KU, sign me up now.

During the tour, I found out about KU's early-entry engineering program. I liked the idea of getting a head start on my engineering career, so that sealed the deal for me. In the summer of 1983, I became an engineering student at KU. It was great to get an early taste of college life, living in a dorm, taking classes, and feeling out the lay of the land with about thirty other early-entry students and advanced high-school students from Kansas City as well. KU even had recreational activities for us to enjoy during our downtime.

Some of my fondest memories came from that summer. The hot summer nights of dancing and roller skating out on the campus, playing basketball on the courts outside, flirting with all the girls, trying to learn how to two-step (all the Kansas City, Missouri, girls knew how but not the ones from Kansas). Between the learning and the fun, it was an exhilarating transition to what would become one of the most transformative periods of my life.

The Scientific Method

At KU, I was a resident assistant in Oliver Hall during my sophomore year so my room and board were taken care of. But during my other years as an undergraduate Dad would pay my monthly dorm "rent" and send me $20 per month for spending money. He recommended I not get a car in college because he thought having one could get me in trouble more easily. Since I couldn't buy a car without his help, I agreed.

Though my studies stretched me further than I'd ever gone before academically, I loved it. College, I discovered, has an uncanny way of suddenly opening the mind to new and previously unfathomable thoughts. I was learning more about computers, technology, and the scientific method than I'd ever thought possible. But this new way of thinking also meant I was opened to entertaining more intellectual doubts about things I had once taken for granted—like the existence of God.

During my years of teen rebellion, there were some questions in my mind regarding the reality of God and the life, death, and resurrection of His Son, Jesus. But somehow, even as I was messing up supremely, I knew He was real. I just figured He didn't want to be around me while I was having my worldly fun. Now, however, I began questioning whether God was around at all. Science seemed to poke holes in this notion of a literal, six-day creation of the world. What about Darwin? What about the Big Bang? I also wondered about the problem of suffering. Why would a benevolent God allow so much pain, so much grief? Science seemed to present a better case for why the world was this way. It was easier to understand the chaos when you removed the notion of an omnipotent God holding everything together. There would be fewer dots to connect, fewer unanswered questions. When you just accept the idea that the world came to be through a random but elaborately precise set of natural occurrences, it frees the mind to think more rationally, more scientifically.

During my last year of high school, my brother George got involved in a charismatic campus ministry at K-State called Maranatha. He rededicated his life to the Lord, and we all saw an amazing change in his demeanor. I even began feeling guilty when he'd come around. My sister Mary and I both noticed how different George looked; it was almost as if he were glowing.

George had been a dedicated runner in high school on the cross-country team. He won the two-mile relay in the state championships and had a little success in community college as well before transferring to K-State. When he was a high-school senior, I was a freshman, and I recall being inspired to go out for cross-country because of George's example. Except that, I wasn't as disciplined as George, so my friends used to kid me because I'd skip practices to go fishing at the river or at Milford Lake. My teammates would ask, "Where'd Andrew go?" And someone would say, "That dude's gone fishing!" But George was committed.

At one point, he took me to see *Chariots of Fire* in the hope of inspiring me to work harder. I remember sitting in the theater and feeling truly moved by the lives of the British runners Harold Abrahams and Eric Liddell during the 1924 Olympics. Abrahams, a Jew, ran as a way of proving his humanity to an anti-Semitic society. Liddell ran for the glory of God, and in one powerful scene declares, "I believe that God made me for a purpose [to serve Him]. But He also made me fast, and when I run, I feel His pleasure." When Liddell decided that he would not run on the Sabbath because of his faith, it made me wonder about the commitments in my life. I wasn't going to church or focusing on God during that time in my life, but Liddell's example of taking a stand for his convictions, no matter the cost, challenged me to examine my own choices. Could I ever make such a sacrifice for a higher purpose?

Before I left for college, George had somehow arranged for the JC Free Methodist Church to give me a Bible in a modern translation, even though I hadn't been there consistently in years. The

Bible was a New American Standard edition (prior to that, I had only read the Bible in the King James Version), and it was the one I had with me now at KU.

While my science classes had raised doubts in my mind about God, it also caused me to start reading my Bible again. Suddenly I was rereading stories I hadn't thought about since I was a child. I was reading the Bible to convince myself, once and for all, that it was simply a collection of myths and fables. But I could not get away from its authority and relevance.

A passage that stood out, in particular, was the parable of the Prodigal Son. I could identify with the son's quest for freedom and pleasure, but also the sense of emptiness and regret that came following his period of wanton living. What I had never fully noted before was how enthusiastically the father welcomed him home. At once, I recognized the story as an allegory of God's love. For many reasons, including my relationship with my dad and the sometimes-legalistic teachings of my old church, I had never thought of God that way before. The Prodigal's father wasn't sitting at home in his absence, thinking of ways to punish his son and make his life miserable if he ever returned home. He was praying for his son's well-being, longing for his safe return. He rejoiced when he saw his son in the distance. And this was how God saw me. He wasn't mad; he hadn't cut me off. He longed for my return. He *loved* me.

"Too Much Bible"

I became fast friends with an African American guy named Leroy Armstrong, a senior in the electrical engineering program. Leroy was shorter than me but large in the confident manner he carried himself. He was preparing to graduate and I was only an entering freshmen, but that didn't make a difference. We connected right away. We first met during a man-to-man battle on the basketball court. He held his own, and we became frequent competitors on the court from then on.

Leroy (who, after a stint as an engineer, went on to become a pastor in Dallas) had been a part of the African American chapter of Campus Crusade for Christ that met on the KU campus. After one hard-fought battle on the ball court, Leroy invited me and a bunch of the other students to attend Sunday worship at the church he attended. Victory Bible Church was a relatively new congregation in Lawrence. The pastor, Leo Barbee Jr., had led Faithful Baptist Church in Lawrence (not its real name), before he was chased out by the deacons because, the story goes, "he was preaching too much Bible." That should give you an idea of what the services were like at Victory Bible the first Sunday I went. Pastor Barbee, sporting an athletic frame and an Afro peppered with gray, was a dynamic communicator who presented the gospel in a clear and compelling manner that I'd never experienced before.

Pastor Barbee's message clarified things for me and untangled some of the knots of confusion that had settled in my mind during my years at JC Free Methodist. Yes, God hates sin. But He always loves the sinner. We deserve the penalty of sin, which is death. But Jesus paid the penalty; He died for our sins past, present, and future. That kind of teaching, along with the parable of the Prodigal Son and a copy of *The Four Spiritual Laws* that George had given me, began to free me from years of guilt, doubt, and apathy.

I remember reading the words of Jesus from Matthew 11:28–30:

> "Come to Me, all who are weary and heavy-laden, and I will give you rest. Take My yoke upon you and learn from Me, for I am gentle and humble of heart, and you shall find rest for your souls. For My yoke is easy and My burden is light."

I reflected on that high school feeling of not being at peace within myself, not being at rest. Now it was as if Jesus were personally speaking to me through the Scripture: "I will give you rest, if you let Me control your life and learn from Me."

Then Pastor Barbee announced, "If there's anyone here who has made that decision to come to Him, stand up now."

I'd once been so close to Jesus, I said to myself. *Now He was wel-coming me back.*

When I stood up, I knew it was the Holy Spirit enabling me to respond. Before then, I would've never done such a thing in front of my friends. But now, like Eric Liddell in *Chariots of Fire,* I understood what a commitment to God really meant.

I was determined to follow Jesus wherever He called me, no matter what.

CHAPTER 7

Recovery Mode

On the night of my Rebirth Day—the Sunday that I stood up at Victory Bible Church to recommit my life to Christ—I knelt down at my bedside in Joseph R. Pearson Hall and prayed, "Lord, from now on, I'm going to base my relationship with you on what you've done and what you said in the Bible, not on my feelings or my performance."

I gave thanks to God for all He had done for me that day, and during all those years when I did my best to ignore Him. Then I added, "Lord, if I'm able to live a Christian life, it's going to have to be through You. I tried before in my own strength, and it didn't work."

Suddenly, I saw God proving Himself to me more each day. It wasn't that He had been hiding or withholding His blessings from me before; it's that I started paying attention again. I arose early for morning walks across the campus. I especially enjoyed watching the ducks swim around Potter Lake. It was like taking a little child to the zoo for the first time and seeing the giraffes and tigers through his eyes; everything seemed so vivid and alive. My senses danced at the reception of each sensation—the singing birds, the moist dew, the rustling leaves, the crisp morning breeze, the fresh scent of pine.

Life was alive again.

Designed for Discipleship

When George found out that I had recommitted my life to the Lord, he sent me a small book called *Growing in Christ*. It was Bible study "for New and Growing Christians" by the Navigators Christian ministry. I didn't know anything about the Navigators at that time, but I went through the book, memorizing the Bible verses it highlighted, and soaked in a lot of foundational principles of the Christian faith.

After successfully making it through KU's early-entry program, I moved to the sixth floor of Templin Hall, an all-male dormitory. In the hallway one evening, I met a guy from the opposite wing of the dorm. His name was Russ Schuller.

Russ was a grad student who, I discovered, also was a Christian. I chatted with him into the wee hours of the night while standing in the doorway of his dorm room. At some point, I noticed some intriguing pictures of Russ pinned to his bulletin board. After asking him about them, he told me they were pictures of him in Australia with a group of people he had met during a short-term mission trip there with the Navigators. When he said "Navigators" and "mission trip," my eyes lit up. I excitedly told him about how I had recently recommitted my life to God.

Russ, it turns out, was a campus leader with the Navigators. He paused for a moment, and then said, "I wasn't planning to do this unless God sent me someone who was really hungry to know about Him, but I want to start a Bible study in the dorm. Would you be interested?"

My eyes lit up even more. "Yeah, that sounds good," I exclaimed, explaining to him how eager I was to learn more about God. I had a lot of wasted years to make up for.

Soon, my roommate, Antoine Lawrence, from East St. Louis,

and another guy from the sixth floor named Jeff Huskerson joined Russ and me for a weekly Wednesday-night Bible study. We started by going through the *Designed for Discipleship* series by the Navigators. The study was like an answer to my prayers. God knew I would need brothers in my dorm to help me stay on course, and these guys were wonderful partners in the faith.

Russ finished his degree after that semester, and so Mike Jordahl, the new Navigators campus representative, stepped in to fill the vacancy and take over leadership of the Bible study. Mike offered to meet with me one-on-one to pass on spiritual disciplines someone had passed on to him. My spiritual "lightbulb" continued to burn brightly, and somehow I knew God had this planned to help me learn the things I neglected to learn back in fifth grade from Pastor Terry. How the words of Pastor Terry rang true, "If at first you don't succeed, read the directions." At last, I was learning to "read the directions" God gave me in the Bible.

Different Flavors

Antoine and I were the only blacks involved in Navigators on the KU campus. This wasn't a big deal in general, but we occasionally felt a bit self-conscious during the larger Navigator events that were dominated by white faces. Growing up in a mixed-race family, attending a mostly white church as a child and a multiracial high school as a teen conditioned me for moving between different cultures. It also helped that I got involved in another organization specifically for African American students. Pastor Leo Barbee Jr., whose church I now attended regularly, helped lead a campus ministry called Harambee (Swahili for "let us pull together").

In a sense, I lived a kind of dual life. Harambee was an African American extension of the Baptist Student Union; and Navigators, of course, was predominantly white. It became my weekly ritual to attend both meetings. Harambee fed my social and cultural needs, while the Navigators' focus on systematic Bible study deepened my intellectual grasp of the Scriptures. Both ministries stressed intentional discipleship—just in different flavors. And both were invaluable to my development as a young Christian.

I went on a variety of summer trips with the Navigators student group. One year we traveled to a Christian ranch in Colorado, where we camped out in the mountains, played games, and managed to squeeze in a little Bible study, too. Another summer took me to the South Side of Chicago, which was fascinating because it was so rare for me to see other African Americans in the Navigators. But I learned there had been a strong black movement of the Navigator ministry at University of Illinois Champaign-Urbana led by a Chicago brother named Bob Price, who is now a theology professor at Northern Seminary in Illinois. I was so excited to see black people who were involved in the same kind of discipleship ministry that I was a part of.

The next summer found us heading to yet another Navigator training program, but this one happened to be located at the New Tribes Missions language institute in Camdenton, Missouri. While there, I met a missionary named Wade Ebersol, who was studying to go to Papua New Guinea. Our group watched a slideshow showing a community of indigenous people in Papua New Guinea who had never heard the story of Jesus and the gospel in their native language. They desperately wanted a translation of the Bible, so they could read and hear the gospel in their own language. That slide presentation made a big impact on me. As it concluded, and lights were flipped back on, I hoped no one would see the tears welling in my eyes. I said quietly, "Lord, if You want me to go I would like to do that, so that people can know about You."

Trips like those, along with the one-on-one discipleship that I received from people like Mike Jordahl and Pastor Barbee, showed me the importance of investing in the lives of others. I experienced firsthand the profound influence an older mentor could have on an eager and receptive college student.

Failure Isn't Fatal

Overall, my undergraduate career was an eventful one, a time of both growth and recovery. When a computer's hard drive becomes corrupt and crashes, one way to restore its contents is to access the computer in recovery mode, which enables you to, in effect, go back to an earlier time before its contents were damaged and restore them to that unspoiled state. Similarly, I needed to go back and recover my zeal both as a student and as a Christian.

Because I came into KU through the summer engineering early-entry program, I zipped ahead in math, taking Calculus II and Differential Equations my freshman year. I was on the academic fast track from the beginning. There were, however, a few bumps along the way.

I reconnected with Kara Mills, the pretty Miss Teen of Kansas whom I had met during that campus preview, and much to my joy and excitement she became my girlfriend. Not surprisingly, I wasn't quite prepared for the distractions of having a girlfriend in college and the corresponding social activities. It was so easy to drift into daydreaming about Kara as I tried to do my lab assignments.

Studying regularly became a struggle. I was such a perfectionist that I'd worry more about having my desk neat than getting my homework done, and no one was there reminding me that I needed to get my homework done because that was the best way to prepare for the tests, which were far more difficult than the high school variety.

It all came to a head when I got a D in Differential Equations during my spring semester. I literally cried when I showed my dad the report card while beginning my summer break. My sister Jeanne later told me that D was like a turning point for me. She saw how deeply it affected me, and how I reasserted myself as a student and worked much harder after that.

Later that year, during one of many Navigators conferences, a Bible teacher named Lorne Sanny was preaching full tilt on the topic of leadership when he digressed briefly to invoke one legendary leader's profound words. "Folks, this isn't in the Bible, but it's basically biblical," Sanny said. He then shared the quote from Winston Churchill that literally changed the way I thought about school—and life—from that day forward: "Success is never final. Failure is seldom fatal. But it's courage that counts."

Churchill's words, along with that D in Differential Equations, would define the rest of my career as a student. It would also become the model for how I approach everything I do. It reminded me that having potential doesn't guarantee fulfilled potential, and that I needed to do what I could do to fulfill the talents that God gave me.

I soon made the difficult decision of breaking up with Kara. I realized that the physical feelings that I had for her were holding me back from giving my all, both academically and spiritually. Engineering would require too much of my focus, I decided. What's more, I would always feel guilty in church on Sunday mornings after being out with Kara late the night before. Though Kara and I were never involved sexually, I could sense it would be only a matter of time before we had no other direction in which to go. At first unconsciously, I sought for ways to end our relationship. I finally found my way out via the future "King of Pop." Kara wanted to go to a Michael Jackson concert. I acted jealous and told her I wanted to break up. It was a lame excuse from someone who had "cold feet," but it was something I had to do.

More than anything else, I felt God wanted me to learn to focus on my spiritual relationship with Him rather than a physical relationship with someone else.

I graduated "Magna-Thank-Ya-Lawdy" from the University of Kansas in 1988. As with most engineering grads, my first priority after school was to find a well-paying job, but I also wanted to continue in ministry work. For that reason, I signed up for a short-term mission trip to Manupari, Bolivia. The trick was finding a job that would allow me to take part of the summer off for the trip.

CHAPTER 8

Anitra

My mission trip to a jungle in Bolivia was profoundly moving. I came home armed with my long slide presentations for everyone to watch. I now understood short-term missionaries' passion. The people I met and the things I experienced in that South American country left a lasting impression on me, along with a taste of reverse culture shock when I came back to the U.S.

Our group of about twelve spent most the time in northwest Bolivia along the Manupari River. The Manupari, which eventually flows into the Amazon, is a beautiful body of winding water bordered by an exotic expanse that gave the aura of a little jungle paradise. But the beauty was balanced with the reality of the region, as the river was populated with piranhas and alligators, with anaconda snakes nearby. This gave all of us a healthy respect for the wild, even as we washed our bodies and laundry in the bustling river. As long as no one bled in the water, we wouldn't have to worry about the piranhas. At least that's what they told us.

The most memorable moments were spent interacting with the Araona people, who made their home in the headwaters of the Manupari River. The missionaries were working to translate portions of the Bible into the Araona language. The Araona people seemed interested in learning how to read and write these stories in their language while also learning to speak Spanish as well. They wanted to find a way, themselves, to climb out of "the box" that held them back from true salvation and education.

Our mission team worked to build a house out of mud and sticks for a new missionary couple. These people didn't have much compared to what we had in North America, but their faces were always lit up with warm smiles. When I first got off the plane at the mission, the children rubbed my skin. They had never seen a missionary with brown skin that was similar to their own skin tone.

Upon returning from Bolivia, I thought seriously about enrolling in a Bible college or seminary to become a tribal missionary. But when I spoke to one of the missionaries who had led our trip to Bolivia, he told me, "Andrew, I think you need to go out and get some work experience first. You have a lot of head knowledge, but you need to experience life where the rubber meets the road."

I swallowed my pride and acknowledged to myself that he was probably right. So, I accepted a position upon graduation as the purchased material quality engineer at AlliedSignal Aerospace Company in Kansas City, Missouri. The company later became a part of the Honeywell Corporation.

Graduating with a bachelor's degree in electrical engineering in 1988 landed me a job that paid $30,000 a year, which was pretty good back then and a lot more than my dad had ever made. That's one of the reasons why I would become so passionate about encouraging others to consider getting an education in technology and the sciences. It can literally transform a person's life vocationally and economically, especially if that person is a first-generation college graduate like I was.

Down from the Mountain

Working at AlliedSignal was a surprisingly difficult adjustment. In college, I had a lot of friends both from the engineering program and from my involvement in Navigators, Harambee, and at Victory Bible Church. I frankly had not anticipated the intense feelings of loneliness and loss I would experience as I left behind those close relationships to launch out on my own.

Because I worked with various suppliers, I had to travel regularly. Since AlliedSignal was a contractor for the Department of Energy, and the company made nonnuclear parts for nuclear weapons, all employees had to get a security authorization called a "Q Clearance." It was one of the highest levels of security clearance that civilians could get, and it enabled us to look at classified information if we ever had to. And they had this area called "the red badge area" for people who hadn't gotten their security clearance, because basically the FBI would have to go talk to all your friends, go to your hometown, ask if you were involved in drugs or was there anything that people could use against you to bribe you for information. And I think on my application I put that I had used drugs before. So someone told me that was probably why it took so long for me to clear. While I was in the red badge area people would go there and just play cards or whatever, and they would do some work, but they couldn't be allowed in the area where they could possible see classified information. So I would travel a lot. Again, that contributed to my struggles with my loneliness and stuff.

I rented an apartment with Antoine, my buddy from KU, who worked at AlliedSignal until he moved out to get married. I later moved in with a coworker who lived in a Kansas City suburb.

Being away from the support and accountability of other Christian men also left me vulnerable to an unexpected temptation. At one point Mike Jordahl talked to me about how a large percentage of college students struggle with addiction to lustful thoughts and actions. I thought that only applied to others because I had worked out a great routine of celibacy by keeping busy with my engineering studies and spending time with my Christian friends. At the time, I couldn't believe a Christian would fall prey to such a thing, especially since it had never been a temptation for me. But something changed after I moved to Kansas City.

After five years of sustained one-to-one spiritual mentoring, or discipleship, I was coming down off a mountaintop. And now, for the first time, I began struggling in those areas. Thankfully, I was now a lot more secure in my faith. My years with the Navigators and Harambee had taught me the central importance of prayer and Scripture memorization. Verses such as 1 Corinthians 10:13 (KJV) looped in my head: "There hath no temptation taken you but such as is common to man: but God is faithful, who will not suffer you to be tempted above that ye are able; but will with the temptation also make a way to escape, that ye may be able to bear it."

Though I would stumble numerous times, giving in to the temptations of lustful thoughts, I was able to regroup and start again. In my heart, I clung to the truth of God's Word. In my mind, the quote I had chosen as a motto for recovering from my academic mishaps rang true for matters of personal purity of thought and action: "Success is never final. Failure is seldom fatal. But it's courage that counts." I finally was able to understand my adventures and misadventures in the Christian life as a journey of learning, over and over, how God can give me victory in those areas where I'm most weak.

Lessons in Loneliness

Part of my loneliness, I now believe, was God nudging me to start thinking about dating and marriage. The Navigators and Harambee had placed a strong emphasis on sexual purity and accountability in relationships. Throughout my time at KU, I was drilled with that kind of teaching. Consequently, in spite of myself, whenever I'd start thinking seriously about a girl, my head would echo with the voices of Mike Jordahl and Pastor Barbee telling me to guard my heart from lust and to pray specifically for what I wanted in a wife. I became determined, no matter what, that I would only pursue a romantic relationship if God made unavoidably clear that I should.

After my clumsy breakup with Kara Mills (was Michael Jackson really worth getting jealous over?), I rarely dated again at KU. My focus shifted to my studies and my faith, along with getting to know persons of the opposite sex in fun, group settings.

Ah, but there was one heartbreaking exception. During my sophomore and junior years, I developed a crush on Amy Patterson (again, the name has been changed). She was a white girl whom I had met through Navigators. We became good friends, often chatting late into the night about God and life. She told me about her struggles with friends and family, and I would try to encourage her. But when I finally mustered the courage to ask her out, I sensed a strange tension.

Amy stood me up when I tried to meet her in Kansas City to either go ice skating or to a movie. I had brought some of my family to meet her. But when I tried to meet up with her unsuccessfully, I experienced one of those awkward moments of self-awareness. Amy didn't even have to say it outright. The excuse for not being able to meet me was clear enough. I think it had something to do with her dad not wanting her to date a black man, and she was caught in the middle. At least that's what I was led to surmise.

Most of the time, I existed at KU blissfully unconcerned about racial differences. I wasn't color-blind, by any means. I recognized the amazing diversity of races and cultures on campus. On the other hand, I also understood that racism was alive and well, even two decades after the zenith of Martin Luther King Jr. and the civil rights movement. Still, obsessing about race did not seem like a practical way to accomplish my academic goals, nor did it help me in my friendships with others. There was plenty to occupy one's mind without borrowing that kind of worry. But suddenly, I had to remind myself that not everyone was comfortable with the idea of a person with my skin color dating his white daughter. This was the stuff we didn't talk about at our Navigators meetings. I always felt left out when I'd see couples start to meet potential mates at the Navigators conferences. I kind of felt like Adam before Eve. There was no one who looked like me in that circle. I began regretting breaking up with Kara.

After graduation, my brother George and his wife, Trudy, introduced me to a young woman from their church named Naomi Cannon. Naomi was half black, half Japanese, and extremely pretty. What's more, she wanted to be a missionary! After meeting her, I said, "Lord, she must be the one, because we both want to be missionaries."

But I soon discovered that I wasn't the only suitor trying to win Naomi's affections. In fact, she had lots of men pursuing her. Yet, she was not particularly affected by all that attention. Instead, she focused on doing God's work—which, I must confess, made her all the more desirable.

Naomi wound up taking a short-term mission trip to England. When I asked if I could come visit her, she said, "Sure, but you do realize that we can only be friends, right?"

Ouch! In a world filled with pain and disappointment, I'm not sure anything stings more than the infamous "just friends" pronouncement from a woman you think you love. Despite Naomi's clear rejection, it took me a long time to get the message that she really didn't think I was the one for her. I wrote her while she was away in England and never got a letter in return. I was devastated. But I soon got over it.

Who's That Girl?

In Kansas City I attended Paseo Baptist Church, named for Paseo Boulevard, where it was located. Oddly enough, it was the first time I had ever attended a traditional African American church. Though Pastor Barbee's church back in Lawrence had been mostly black, there were still a good number of white attendees in the mix. And it was cross-cultural enough in tone that it felt like all the other white or mixed-raced institutions that I had belonged to since I was a kid in Junction City.

Paseo, however, was a bona fide "Black Baptist Church," with the music, preaching, and long services to match. The choir "sang," and even though the preacher didn't "hoop," there was the electric sense that old-school praise and preaching could break out at any time. I started going to Paseo Baptist because Pastor Barbee was a good friend of Paseo's senior pastor, Charles Briscoe. Dr. Briscoe was an illustrious and influential leader, both in the church and the local community. When he came to the church in 1967, he instituted an ambitious Bible education program that helped make Paseo members, from preschool to senior citizen, some of the most biblically literate Christians in the city. His civic accomplishments were equally noteworthy. In addition to launching several community outreach programs, he was voted the first African American president of the Kansas City Board of Education. By the time he retired in 2003, he had left an indelible mark on Kansas City, and on people across the nation. Pastor Barbee and many others counted him as a friend and mentor. Indeed, Tony Evans, the renowned preacher and author from Dallas, calls Dr. Briscoe "a pastors' pastor." And so it was with great anticipation that I took Pastor Barbee's advice and visited Paseo Baptist Church.

Boy, am I glad I did. The teaching was excellent, and the members were gracious. On my first Sunday, there were about 500 people in attendance. Initially, it did feel weird to be attending a traditional black church. But I quickly adjusted, especially after I saw the gorgeous young woman with the long hair.

It was around my sixth month at the church and Dr. Briscoe, as was his custom, had concluded his sermon with an altar call, that time for people to publicly make a decision to believe in Jesus Christ as their own personal Savior from separation from God and begin a new, personal relationship with Him. I saw the young woman slowly making her way to the front of the sanctuary. Her hair was silky and dark; it flowed down her back like an ebony waterfall. Her shoulders appeared broad (which, I would learn later, was the result of shoulder pads in her dress, which was the style back then). She wore a blue and white dress that perfectly accented her flawless, caramel-colored skin.

As I admired her beauty, I had to remind myself that I was in church—and that this woman was in the process of surrendering her life to Jesus Christ. I quietly prayed for her, as well as the other handful of people who went forward that morning. But especially her. My heart was going "pitter-patter."

It took me few weeks to finally approach her. After having been rejected by Naomi, I was quite apprehensive about seriously pursuing anyone. So I watched her from a distance, eventually learning her name—Anitra Byrd—and her story. I was later to find out that her stepmom and stepgrandmother attended the church. She had graduated from the University of Missouri–Kansas City with a degree in psychology and worked downtown helping low-income families, refugees, and single mothers. She had worked her way through college while sometimes having to care for both her mother and brother. She rode the city bus to her college classes down Troost Avenue, the unofficial dividing line between white and black Kansas City.

In some ways, her spiritual journey had been similar to my own. She had grown up going to a Church of God in Christ. She liked the people there, but they often made her feel spiritually inferior because she didn't "speak in tongues," that special language some say only comes when a person has been filled with the Holy Spirit. It's not that she didn't want to; she just never "received the gift." She eventually left that church, and for a while she abandoned faith altogether—until she accepted her stepgrandmother's invitation to visit her church, Paseo Baptist.

When I finally decided to speak to her, she had become an usher welcoming church patrons and visitors with a smile and a church program outlining the worship service. She wore the traditional black suit, white shirt, and white gloves that the position required, but I remember thinking how young she looked next to the older ladies. I intentionally entered down her aisle that morning. As she handed me the church bulletin, I said, "Hi, my name's Andrew. What's yours?" She looked down at the nametag on her lapel and replied, "Anitra." I thought, *Ah, man, I blew it. She thinks I can't read!*

Actually, I would later discover that she was similarly embarrassed. *Why am I looking at my nametag?* she recalled thinking. *He's going to think I'm being sarcastic.*

After that, we would see each other in church, but she would disappear right after the service. Until one Sunday I managed to catch her immediately after the closing prayer to ask her out. To my great relief and joy, she said yes.

Stumbling into Love

Our first date was to the Country Club Plaza in downtown Kansas City. The plaza is filled with exquisite Spanish architecture, a plethora of lovely fountains, and dozens of quaint restaurants and shops. Horse-drawn carriages circled the area, and scores of tourists and couples added to the charm and romance of the place.

This led to my second miscalculation (I'll get to the first one in a moment). With all the nice, classy restaurants on the plaza, where did I take this beautiful young woman whom I had waited a half year to ask out?

McDonald's.

I know. Not a very savvy move. But it wasn't that I was trying to be cheap. It was simply a reflection of the way I was thinking about dating during that time. And I must admit, I was probably thinking too hard. Anitra went along with it, but I soon found out that she was not too happy with me.

Which leads to my *first* miscalculation. As we dined over Big Macs and milkshakes, Anitra informed me that she was perturbed by something I had said to her on the phone days earlier.

During that call, I thought it would be wise to let her know that I wasn't looking for a girlfriend or a serious relationship; I just wanted to be friends. After she hung up with me, she immediately dialed her friends to vent her rage over my presumptuous statement. "What's he talking about?" she told them. "How would he even know I would want to be his girlfriend anyway?"

I now understand my error, my tendency to take things too seriously too soon. Years of Navigators meetings can do that to a guy.

It turned out Anitra had recently ended an earlier relationship. So we both had reasons to take it slowly. But as we talked and hung out more, the chemistry between us became undeniable. And I found myself thanking God for the chance to get to know this smart, beautiful, and godly woman. I had fallen into what's best described as infatuation with other girls before, but now I understood those relationships and near relationships for the incomplete relationships that they really were.

This time was different. Dare I say it? This time I was truly falling in love.

CHAPTER 9

Bringing Good Things to Life

Six months after our first date, Anitra and I started talking about marriage. And then . . . I got cold feet.

It wasn't anything Anitra had said or done. I knew she was a caring woman, who would make an excellent wife and mother. What I wasn't so sure about were my own calling and purpose. Could I really love this person in the way a husband should love his wife, or was I simply in love with her intelligence and looks and the fact that she made me feel special?

There was also an enduring tug on my heart to become a missionary. As much as I tried to deny it, it was still there. I kept thinking, *Missions, missions, missions.*

I recalled one Sunday at Paseo Baptist when a guest speaker named Brian Johnson came through. He told of how he was a former executive assistant at GM in Detroit who had answered the call to be a missionary to Liberia, West Africa. As a GM exec, he had traveled all over the world. He hung out with wealthy business people who would take private jets around the globe just to play golf. His lifestyle afforded him access to the highest levels of leisure and luxury. Yet his life felt empty. Then he answered the call to missions. "Now, I have the best job in the world," he said. "Reaching people for Jesus Christ." I could see the joy and passion in his eyes, and it reignited my fervor for missions. I started thinking about going to Bible college again.

After that, I would drop occasional remarks to Anitra about what a future with me might look like. "Would you be willing to live in a jungle?" I'd ask her.

"Well," she'd say, "it would be hard. But yes, I would." And I could tell she was genuinely willing.

Anitra was an amazingly loyal person. Even though she hadn't experienced the particular brand of discipleship training that I'd gone through with the Navigators, I could tell she really loved God and was loyal to Him in her heart—much more loyal to Him than I had ever been. Though I had a lot of head knowledge, I knew my devotion wasn't as steady as hers.

I was, however, good at overthinking stuff. Whenever the topic of marriage would come up, the questions would flood my brain: Do I really want to tie myself down to one place, one woman? I tried to hide my fears about marriage by reasons and excuses that sounded spiritual and pious. If I were going on the mission field, shouldn't I leave myself open to the possibility of Bible college for more training? What if God led me back to Bolivia or some other distant country? Was I just complicating future decisions by allowing my relationship with Anitra to grow deeper?

Three Different Directions

Besides Anitra, there was really nothing to hold me in Kansas City. After nearly two years at AlliedSignal, I had begun feeling restless.

I knew there was more to life than being a purchased material quality engineer. Frankly, it was boring. It was more old-school electromechanical science than high-tech engineering. My passion for computers and software was not being nurtured at all. I realized I was only there for the paycheck, that it was a dead-end job for me. I saw the employees who had worked there for years. They made a good living, for sure. But none of them seemed truly fulfilled. And I realized I was becoming just like them.

I felt pulled in at least three different directions. What, I wondered, was my true calling? The mission field, computer engineering, or marriage?

As I wrestled with all of this, I was reminded of the advice of a national Navigators leader who spoke to the KU chapter one year. His name was Ray Ho. He was Chinese American and a dynamic Bible teacher. Ray encouraged students who were interested in foreign missions to get their master's degrees in a secular field. He explained that many countries were not open to traditional missionaries, but they will permit entry to professionals such as engineers and people with master's degrees who possess useful skills.

"You could be a tentmaker missionary," Ray said, referring to the popu-lar method of evangelism promoted by the Navigators. The concept of "tentmaking" comes from the strategy used by the apostle Paul. While serving as a missionary in the Greek city of Corinth, Paul supported himself by making tents (Acts 18:3). The benefits were twofold: By earning an income through a trade, Paul did not put an added financial burden on the local church; plus, he was able to rub shoulders with the people of the community.

I thought about Ray's words, my call to missions, and my passion for computer science, and then it became clear: I would get my master's degree in computer engineering and become a tentmaker missionary.

"What About Us?"

Anitra and I had just finished walking along the Country Club Plaza in Kansas City when I told her about my decision to go back to KU for graduate school. Her initial response was polite and gracious. She had learned to go with the ebb and flow of my frequently shifting emotions.

"That's great, Andrew," she said. But she jarred me out of my tunnel vision with a question that compelled me to talk about the subject I'd hope to avoid: "What about us?"

I froze.

"What about *our* future?"

What could I say? I knew I loved Anitra. But could I love her the way a husband should love his wife? Did I care about her enough to delay my sense of calling? What's more, wouldn't it be selfish or disobedient for me to put marriage before God's call to missions? Or was I just trying to make excuses for being scared of committing to one woman for the rest of my life?

I took her hands into mine and forced myself to look into her brown eyes. Her skin felt so soft. "Anitra, this is hard for me," I said, my voice quivering. "I really love you as a person. But I can't say 100 percent that I'm ready right now for . . . "

I could see the tears welling up in her eyes. I gently gripped her hands tighter.

"I'm sorry, Anitra, but I think we should break up."

The rest of that night is a blur. It certainly wasn't a walk in the park, despite our location. There were tears, polite anger, and an awkward good-bye. I left her that evening not knowing whether she would ever speak to me again. I called our church friends Ray and Robin McKelvy to explain what had happened. I had tears in my eyes as I shared my confused emotions. "I don't want to lead her on if I can't be 100 percent sure that I am ready to be married to her," I explained.

Ray and Robin were kind enough to listen. But I still felt like a wretch.

Back to the Future

In 1991 I left AlliedSignal and returned to KU's School of Engineering, this time as a graduate student pursuing a master's in electrical engineering with a focus on software development and artificial intelligence. I felt rejuvenated to be back in an academic environment. I didn't realize how much I had missed it. That first semester my roommate was an undergraduate architecture major named Devan Case. We lived off campus in a house owned by his dad, who was a successful St. Louis entrepreneur and a devoted Christian who was a benefactor of several African American ministries.

During the spring semester, I led a Navigators Bible study for a group of African American students that included Devan, his younger brother Anthony, and two other undergrads. Eight years earlier, I was the wide-eyed freshman student, eager to deepen his Christian faith. Suddenly, I was occupying the role that men like Mike Jordahl and Leroy Armstrong once filled for me. Some nights, as I prayed and studied with my guys, a quiet smile would creep onto my face. It was a smile of personal gratitude for all the faithful mentors who had invested in me through the years. Now I was passing on their gift—of being a role model and making disciples— to another generation.

One spring evening, I attended an awards banquet for minority engineers. It was an inspiring event that honored KU engineering school alumni who were achieving great things in their profession and society. The returning KU graduates gave all of us young or aspiring engineers a glimpse of what we could accomplish if we stayed focused on our goals.

Mike Shinn was one of the alumni being honored that night. He had attended KU back in the early sixties, when he was a teammate of future NFL running back Gale Sayers. He talked about sharing the football field with Sayers while Sayers was setting Kansas Jayhawks records. Shinn shared about his work with General Electric (GE) where he had spent many years as a corporate recruiter. Through the years, Shinn had helped dozens of young people break into the engineering field at GE. He told the story of growing up in Kansas as the descendant of black farmers. His grandparents owned a farm in Oskalooska, Kansas, and hauled brick and stone to help build KU in the late 1800s. Motivated by the examples of his family, he worked hard to get an education and make something of himself.

Before Shinn graduated from KU, his dad told him, "Whatever you do, you always have to reach back and help other people. You mustn't forget where you're from." And that was the heart of his short acceptance speech.

Later, after the ceremony, I had the chance to chat with Shinn. After I shared a bit of my journey with him, he asked me, "So, what are you doing this summer?"

I told him I didn't know. I knew I needed to earn some extra money, but I wasn't sure whether I could get back on at AlliedSignal or some other company. Shinn smiled, lowered his voice to a loud whisper, and shot back, "Then why don't you come work at GE in Milwaukee?"

I told him I was interested but that I'd need to think about it. However, inside I was doing cartwheels and high fives. It was an answer to prayer, and a great opportunity to build upon my skills.

Once again, it was as if God were saying, "See, this is what I mean, Andrew. If you just make Me first in your life, I will take care of you."

Sweet Reunion

Life was going well—mostly. I loved being back in school. I'd regained my passion for programming computers and developing software. Plus, I was still growing in my Christian faith, preparing myself for God's call on my life. Though I was no longer actively involved with the Navigators, I occasionally met with staff to pray and talk about the Bible. And now I had an excellent summer job lined up at GE. The only thing I didn't have was a girlfriend.

I hadn't spoken to Anitra in months, though I thought about her often, wondering if she'd ever forgive me. Nevertheless, I was confident I made the right decision. God was calling me to ministry, and I couldn't see any other way to follow His lead. It simply wasn't the right timing for a long-term relationship.

This didn't mean I was totally devoid of a social life. In fact, I had even gone out on a few dates with a new young woman. She was smart, attractive, and a computer science major to boot. But even as we were going out, I knew it wasn't right. The bottom line: She wasn't Anitra. Without trying, I now measured every new girl against Anitra; and next to her, in my mind, they were all found wanting.

Then it arrived. A message in the mail from Benola Briscoe, Pastor Briscoe's wife. She had written me a letter that went something like this:

Dear Andrew,

My husband and I pray for you every day. We trust you're doing well at the University of Kansas. Please forgive me if I seem to be interfering in your private business, but this letter comes out of my love and concern for you and Anitra.

Anitra didn't tell me to write this letter, but she's feeling confused. She cares about you deeply, but she doesn't understand what happened between the two of you.

I think it would be good if you talked to her.

Sincerely,
Sister Benola Briscoe

While reading Mrs. Briscoe's letter, it finally registered in my brain just how poorly I had handled things with Anitra. So blinded was I by my questions about the future, that I didn't know how to relate to this special person whom God had given me in the present. I had to swallow my pride and admit that I had made a huge mistake.

I picked up the phone and called Anitra.

"Hello?"

"Hi, Anitra. This is Andrew. How are you?"

There was a brief but obvious silence. "I'm fine. How are you?" I could hear in her voice that she wasn't fine, at least not with me. I could hear the sadness, and perhaps a trace of lingering resentment. Still, I loved hearing her gentle voice.

After a few minutes of awkward small talk and explaining about the letter from Mrs. Briscoe, I told her about a Wycliffe Bible Translators banquet in Lawrence that I had been invited to. "Would you like to go with me?"

She agreed, and drove down the following weekend. When I saw her arrayed in an elegant evening dress, her stunning smile and flowing hair overwhelming my vision, I thought to myself, *Man, Andrew, what were you thinking?*

After the banquet, I took her for a brief stroll across campus. As we walked around Potter Lake, I quietly took her hand.

"Anitra," I said nervously, "I'm sorry for the way I treated you."

Her eyes sparkled in the night air.

"I thought I needed to have everything figured out ahead of time, but I now see that I just need to leave some of those details to God."

"What are you saying, Andrew?"

"I'm saying, I love you. And I want us to be together again."

Her face lit up with a wide grin, even as her eyes filled with tears.

"I have no idea how things will fall into place from here," I said. "But I know that as long as we commit our futures to God, He'll take care of it."

We embraced for a long and wonderful while, and suddenly everything seemed right—school, summer job, the future.

These days, when I counsel young men about relationships, I do not tell them what to do. After all, each situation is different. But I do try to help them establish realistic expectations, to steer them away from that type A impulse of feeling you need to have every jot and tittle of your future worked out before making a commitment to the woman you love. Not only is it impossible, for only God knows the future, but it robs you of the adventure of growing together, of anticipating together, of having faith together in the providence of God to supply all of your needs.

I realized that night that I had been putting God into a box, limiting what I believed He could do. I of all folks should've known better than that, right?

The Eyes of the Lord

Things took off after that night. Anitra and I started talking about marriage again, but this time I was genuinely engaged in the conversation. I took her to California to meet my parents.

At first, I felt a little nervous about introducing Anitra to my family, though I was confident everyone would like her. What made me most ner-vous was not knowing how Anitra would react. I was eager to open up all of my life to the woman I planned to marry, and my family was very important to me. But I didn't want to overwhelm Anitra with our ample family baggage either.

And sure enough, during our visit, Anitra received a firsthand glimpse of one of Momma's extreme bouts with her mental illness. At one point, Momma came out of her room and was behaving very unusually. Dad and I quickly helped her settle down. It frightened Anitra a bit, but she is a sweet and understanding person who took it in stride once she got over the initial spectacle.

I also met Anitra's family again. Her mother and father had divorced when she was a little girl, but they maintained a good relationship. She now lived with her mother. When I'd first started dating Anitra a couple years earlier, I visited her dad to ask his permission. Later, Anitra laughed as she told me that her dad had been surprised by my gesture. "He was like, 'What was he asking *that* for?'" But, she added, he did like me.

Mike Shinn made good on his words and arranged a summer internship for me at GE Medical Systems in Waukesha, Wisconsin, near Milwaukee. Not only did GE grant me exposure to the medical technology industry, but they also gave me signing bonus, a rental car, and paid housing for the summer. It was a wonderful experience, and I gave it everything I had. If I were going to work at any company as an engineer, I knew I wanted it to be a place like GE.

If there were any negative eye-openers from my experience, it was discovering that companies like GE were more likely to hire their engineers from institutions like Stanford, MIT, or a Big Ten school such as Michigan. Before that, I never fully understood that there was such a thing as a hierarchy of schools—and that Kansas didn't make the upper cut. I realized that, on paper, I didn't necessarily have the pedigree those companies were searching for. Nevertheless, God had opened the way for me to get a foot into GE, despite my academic shortcomings. (I have since learned that institutional pedigree can sometimes be used by organizations in making hiring and advancement decisions. But I have also learned that it's not just the school someone attends but what a person does with the education and opportunities that he's been given. The ability to continually listen, analyze, communicate, and learn is far more important than the name on one's degree.)

I returned to Kansas that fall thankful for the GE experience, but also happy to be reunited with Anitra. Seeing her again in person was a sight for my sore eyes. Another gift from my summer away was gaining a fresh certainty that Anitra was the woman with whom I wanted to spend the rest of my life.

When I told my parents that I was thinking about marrying Anitra, my dad was happy for us. But my mom was another story.

"No, you shouldn't marry her," Momma said.

"Why?" I asked, feeling a bit shaken.

"Because you're still in school, and you don't have a job!"

She had a point, of course, and I agreed with her. But Anitra and I had prayed and were trusting God to provide.

I recalled a memory verse that God had impressed upon my heart: "For the eyes of the Lord move to and fro throughout the earth that He may strongly support those whose heart is completely His" (2 Chronicles 16:9).

One thing the Navigators taught me was that there are verses in the Bible that must be read and interpreted from the context in which they were written. However, there are principles that you can glean from almost any passage of Scripture for life application. This is one of the reasons, I believe, the book of Hebrews calls the Word of God "living and active" (4:12). It has ongoing meaning and importance for every life situation.

During this period in my life, that 2 Chronicles passage had become a verse I was clinging to as a promise from God, that if I yield my heart totally to Him, He would strongly support me. What an amazing picture: God is actively scouting out those on the earth whose lives are fully committed to Him—He's looking for them, so that He can strongly support them. It's akin to Nike looking for the next Tiger Woods, a marketable representative whom they can fully support, so that when people see him wearing Nike gear, it advertises the company with impact. God is looking for someone to advertise His glory, someone who's fully committed to Him.

Momma still strongly advised me to "get a job first," but she understood. And I was thankful for her concern.

Anitra and I continued to pray that God would supply our needs. But we were also open to God's timetable. If He wanted us to get married later rather than sooner, that was fine. We waited expecting God to move.

The Lightbulb Goes On

About a week after my conversation with my mom, I received a call from Greg Jones, the Edison Engineering supervisor from GE I had met during my summer internship.

"Andrew, we were so impressed with your work here over the summer that we'd like to offer you a full-time position," Greg said.

I almost dropped the phone.

GE wanted me to enter their Edison Engineering Program, a two-year technical training project that offered rotational assignments and instruction in corporate leadership skills. Greg explained that I could transfer my graduate work to Marquette University in Milwaukee, and GE would pay for my education.

Wow, I said to myself, *this is the answer to our prayers!*

Following that, I had no doubt that God would "strongly support" Anitra and me.

I told Greg that I needed to discuss it with Anitra and would call him back in a couple of days with my answer. But I'm sure the elation in my voice forecast what my response would be.

I was going back to Milwaukee, and soon I would ask Anitra to marry me and join me there.

I had started out earning $700 a month as a graduate assistant at KU, which meant I had very little money. But I also had no debt. My master's program was being funded through a research assistantship and later on by a Patricia Roberts Harris Fellowship, which was great. Unfortunately, I could not use any of those scholarships to buy a ring. Plus, I had contributed most of my savings to the common fund that the Williams siblings had established for moving my parents to California.

I was desperate to get an engagement ring for Anitra, ask her to marry me, and to finally bring a sense of authenticity to all our chatter about engagements and weddings. I could buy something on credit, but it wouldn't have amounted to much and I didn't want to open a door to amassing debt. I needed cash.

I had done my window-shopping and research, and the ring I wanted for Anitra cost about $2,000. So, I asked God to provide the resources—or to downsize my expectations accordingly.

Then a neighbor backed into my 1980 Toyota Corolla hatchback while it was parked in front of the house I was renting. The neighbor's insurance "totaled" the car, even though it only sustained a minor dent on one side. But I was not about to argue—especially after they sent me a check for almost $2,000. Once again, God had come through even though I didn't feel like I deserved it.

I promptly purchased that ring for Anitra and proposed to her one starry evening while we dined at the Skies Rooftop Revolving Restaurant, on the top floor of the Hyatt Regency Hotel in downtown Kansas City. It was an amazing view, both outside the panoramic windows and right in front of me. And when Anitra said yes, my heart skipped a beat, even though we had talked about getting married for several months.

We were both thrilled, but amid our joy we also grasped the magnitude of what lay ahead. From our personal experiences, we both understood that marriage would require a lot of hard work and sacrifice. We were excited about what lay ahead because we had seen God provide in unexpected ways.

CHAPTER 10

"Andrew, We're Not in Kansas Anymore"

"Welcome back to Waukesha," Greg Jones, the Edison Engineering manager, said to me on my first day back at General Electric.

I began my second stint at GE Medical Systems in January of 1992. The Edison Engineering Program was both exhilarating and exhausting. We learned about and helped engineer X-ray machines, CT scanners, MRI scanners, and PET scanners. Diving deep into all that technology was an incredible opportunity to advance my knowledge and expertise as an electrical engineering student. It was like being turned loose on a real-world engineering playground.

Our Edison Engineering class of seven came from a variety of schools, which demonstrated an effort by GE to bring in a diverse set of future engineering leaders. We had three women, including a person of Hispanic descent and two African Americans. Mark was from the University of Michigan and Stanford, Jean was from University of Wisconsin–Milwaukee, Kim was from the Milwaukee School of Engineering, Rebecca was from the University of Wisconsin–Madison and Marquette (where I had transferred to continue working on my master's in electrical and computer engineering), Robert was from the University of Michigan, and Sam was from Michigan State.

We had a fun group that got along well. Jean and Kim always teased Robert about women in the engineering world (or the lack thereof). Sam and I used to joke about nerdy engineering and math stuff like single-value decomposition (I know, you had to be there). And Robert and Mark would always boast about their Michigan football season while I waited to see if KU would win another national basketball championship. We all needed the humor to keep from going crazy! Not only did GE overload our schedules with daily engineering projects, but we also had to work evenings and weekends to complete special Edison Engineering assignments. On top of that, I was completing my master's and would soon get married. In spite of that crazy activity, working at GE with my Edison friends was a time of my life that I will always look back upon with fondness. Everyone was always very supportive of each other and a true delight to work with. I'm thankful that we have remained friends to this day.

During this time, I also stayed in touch Mike Shinn. Even though he was based at the corporate headquarters on the East Coast, he had become somewhat of a long-distance mentor to me.

Tying the Knot

Anitra and I had set our wedding date for April. So, throughout my first few months at GE I diligently sent money back home to help pay for the various wedding details—the photographer, the cake, the tuxedo, the dress. I was only able to travel back to Kansas City a couple times before the wedding, but Anitra and I spent hours talking on the phone—planning, laughing, dreaming. I left most of the aesthetic decisions to Anitra. Frankly, selecting the specific colors of napkins and tablecloths didn't thrill me much. In that way, I suppose you could say it was a mixed blessing that I didn't have to become too involved in the details. Still, I missed Anitra tremendously.

We were finally married on April 18, 1992, four months after getting engaged. Anitra found a dazzling dress that lit up the sanctuary as her dad walked her down the aisle at Paseo Baptist. Mr. Byrd was beaming with pride but was walking down the aisle at, what seemed to me, an unbelievably slow pace. If he had taken one minute longer, I probably would have run down the aisle and grabbed Anitra from him. My brother George, who was my best man, fortunately was finally able to retrieve his tuxedo after locking it and his keys in his running car just before the wedding.

My friends Jeff Huskerson and Antoine Lawrence, who were with me in that first Navigators Bible study nine years earlier, were my groomsmen, along with the rest of my brothers. The sanctuary was filled with wonderful family and friends from every season of our lives: our parents, teachers, classmates, mentors, church family, and former coworkers. I was delighted to see Sharon and David Scoggins, along with Sharon's dad, Mr. Martin, and Juanita Schwab, another Sunday school teacher from the Free Methodist Church in Junction City.

Many of the people in attendance would go on to various levels of national distinction. Carey Casey, who came with his wife, Melanie, was a friend from KU who went on to pastor the influential Lawndale Community Church in Chicago and to work in the national office of the Fellowship of Christian Athletes. Lynda and Mike Randle were there, too. Lynda became a successful gospel musician and now sings with the popular Bill Gaither Band, and Mike, a KU architecture graduate and another protégé of Pastor Barbee, became a pastor himself. Mike, along with Leroy Armstrong, had been a great mentor and role model for me at KU.

And then there were Tony and Lauren Dungy, who were members of Paseo Baptist Church. Tony is known these days as the Super Bowl–winning NFL coach of the Indianapolis Colts, and Lauren is his beloved wife who quietly ministers to the women of the NFL. Anitra and I met the Dungys at Paseo Baptist when Tony was work-

ive-backs coach for the Kansas City Chiefs. As a vol-
 ...ur church's Pioneer Clubs youth ministry, Anitra helped
teach the Dungys' kids Tiara and James. Tony and Lauren would invite young couples over to their home on Friday or Saturday nights to eat pizza, watch the sketch comedy show *In Living Color*, and laugh with abandon. As a loving and committed African American couple, the Dungys were wonderful role models for Anitra and me and many others. We didn't know Tony as a famous football coach, but rather as a quiet but fun-loving person who teased me as I tried learning to play the keyboard for our church's gospel choir, of which Lauren was a member. I also remember all of us playing basketball at nearby Calvary Bible College and the time I almost suffered heat stroke trying to beat Tony in a church tennis tournament held on the Plaza in Kansas City.

There were more serious moments, too. Occasionally, Tony and Lauren would take the young adults from Paseo Baptist bowling. One evening when we were riding in our cars on the way to the bowling alley in Overland Park, Kansas, a carload of white people in the opposite lane was passing us when someone in the car shouted, "Go back to Wyandotte County!" Wyandotte was the county where most of the Kansas City area's black population was concentrated. We laughed it off then, but later the Dungys led us in an honest discussion about the continued reality of racism in America.

The Dungys lived in an affluent suburb of Kansas City. I remember being in awe during my initial visit to their home; it was my first time seeing a house with a three-car garage. But Tony and Lauren were nothing if not generous, both with their resources and time. Not long after we got married, Tony accepted a job as the defensive coordinator of the Minnesota Vikings, and the Dungys moved to Minneapolis and have since moved on to even greater opportunities. But we have continued to keep in touch and pray for them throughout Tony's career. They remain good friends and role models.

In our wedding video, as Anitra and I are exiting the church

Dad, a WWII and Korean War veteran, in his early Army days.

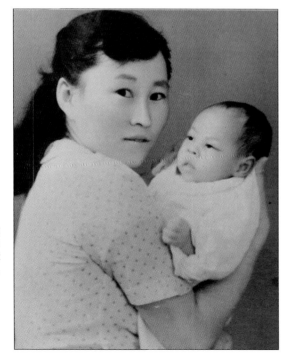

Momma holding my sister Jeanne in a photo sent to my Dad.

Me, two years old, playing with an Army helmet. This is the closest I have to a baby picture.

George, Jeanne, Morgan, Mary, Momma, Me, and Dad on a train car in a Fort Riley, KS park. Robert is not pictured since he's taking the picture.

Momma, Dad, and I in a park in Fort Riley, Kansas.

Dad and my daughter Adrianna as we revisit our former house where we grew up in Junction City, Kansas.

Anitra and I on our wedding day at the Paseo Baptist
Church in Kansas City, Missouri.

The Williams siblings: Back row: George and Andrew
Front row: Morgan, Mary, Jeanne, Robert

Adrianna, Rosa, John, Anitra, and I in December 2006.

Me standing in front of the former Free Methodist Church building in Junction City, Kansas. It is now a Korean church.

My Navigator friends (from left to right):

Back row: Jeff Huskerson, Brian Doerr, Jack Laptad, Matt Layton, Me,
Steve Ashmore.
Front row: Dean Wilson, Wayne Walden, Mike Jordahl, John Schick

My family and I along with Tony and Lauren Dungy (second from left), and
their friend, celebrating their daughter Tiara's graduation from Spelman.

Some of my friends from Harambee and Victory Bible Church: Orrin Gaines, Richawn Buford, and Ornette Gaines.

The SpelBots, with Andrea Lawrence (far left), me, and Dr. Beverly Daniel Tatum (far right), president of Spelman College in Osaka, Japan, getting ready to leave our hotel to compete. Courtesy of Spelman College.

SpelBots 2005 Team: Shinese Noble, Karina Liles, Aryen Moore-Alston, Me, Ebony Smith (white shirt), Ebony O'Neal, Brandy Kinlaw. Courtesy of Spelman College.

The SpelBots AIBO robots (in blue) competing in soccer at the RoboCup 2005 in Osaka, Japan. Courtesy of Spelman College.

after the ceremony, you can hear Lauren yelling from her seat in the balcony: "Anitra! Anitra!" As the church organ plays on, Anitra looks up and waves in her direction. It was one of many sweet moments from that special day.

I was twenty-seven on my wedding day and, by God's grace, still a virgin—at least physically. "Going all the way" had certainly crossed my mind in the past, especially during those hot high school parties and dances. At times when my flesh wanted me to lose my virginity, somehow God protected me from myself. As Anitra and I began married life together, I was thankful for that merciful gift.

Long ago, Pastor Barbee had counseled me to make my future wife an object of my prayers. Well, God answered beyond anything I could've imagined. Now, one of my prayers was that our marriage would be a living illustration of Christ's love and His sacrificial commitment to His bride, the church. I wanted to follow God's principles for marriage to show the world that they are, indeed, the best way. And, recalling the message of 2 Chronicles 16:9, I wanted Anitra and me to advertise His glory and be a witness for Him in everything we do.

Getting to Know Milwaukee

Following a whirlwind honeymoon in Kansas City, we packed all of our belongings into a U-Haul truck and Anitra's car and made the long trip from Kansas City to Milwaukee. Cell phones were not as widespread nor affordable at that point, so we used walkie-talkies to stay in touch while on the road during our nine-hour journey. (Back then, a portable cell phone was as big as an old grade-school lunchbox because of the size of the battery. Thankfully, the engineers eventually figured out how to shrink the technology.)

After getting Anitra settled into our new home, a two-bedroom apartment in New Berlin, a suburb of Milwaukee, we played tourists and visited several of Milwaukee's signature attractions—the lakefront, the downtown landmarks, Marquette. Before I returned to work, I wanted to show her as much of her new city as I could.

Our sightseeing included a tour at the world-famous Miller Brewing Company. Though neither of us were big beer drinkers, it was fascinating to observe the complex process of creating and bottling the beverage.

A sobering reality of Milwaukee—and life in general—revealed itself to us as we interacted with other tourists. At the conclusion of the Miller tour, visitors can sample beer or nonalcoholic alternatives. As we waited, people engaged in small talk about where they were from, where they worked, and so on. We were having a pleasant chat with a middle-aged white woman, until I informed her that I worked at GE. She paused, gave me an odd gaze, and said, "How did you get a job at there? They wouldn't hire my daughter." The astonishment in her voice implied some racial subtext to her question.

"I went to college and applied for the job," I said politely. But I could see in her expression and hear in her tone that she probably viewed me as some undeserving recipient of affirmative action. Was I being overly sensitive? I usually try to give people the benefit of the doubt when it comes to racial incidents; after all, I've had plenty experiences on both sides of the color line. But this woman's body language and look of disdain were unmistakable.

Over time, I had had similar experiences in Milwaukee that left me feeling keenly aware of my skin color. Stray comments, offensive jokes, slow service at restaurants, suspicious looks. I'd witnessed prejudice and segregation in Kansas City, where many of the black sections of town clearly suffered from economic disparity. But Milwaukee's black neighborhoods evinced an even greater sense of isolation and lack of opportunity.

Anitra eventually took a position as a counselor at a social service agency, where she ran a program for pregnant teens, connecting them with mentors, prenatal care, and other helpful resources. Anitra was responsible for hiring and training the agency's staff and volunteers, so she interacted with countless people from the community. At that time, Milwaukee had one of the highest teen pregnancy rates in the nation, especially among black girls, and Anitra encountered many people in Milwaukee's white community who were bitter about it. Some spoke disparagingly of black girls relocating to Milwaukee from Chicago because Wisconsin had a better welfare program. Anitra was often saddened by the racial animosity that she sensed always simmering beneath the surface.

Of course, I was not naïve to the special opportunities that had been extended to me. I was hired at a time when it seemed GE was working to improve diversity among its ranks. But whatever the impetus behind my hiring, I embraced it as a golden opportunity—and one in which I wouldn't have lasted more than a month if I hadn't had the intelligence, skill, and discipline to do the work. I realized then that affirmative action efforts, while not necessarily ideal, were important attempts to equalize social conditions for minority and female members of society who might typically not be given a fair shot at educational and employment opportunities. And the inequality didn't always stem from race and gender; often it was simply due to the fact that people did not have the geographic, familial, or institutional connections that naturally placed them on the radar screens of the top schools and employers.

In GE's Edison Engineering Program, I learned firsthand about the aca-demic pedigree system that our country has constructed based on who went to "the best" schools. When companies select employees based primarily on their pedigree or what school they attended, it becomes a kind of unspoken class system. And this invariably impacts the number of minorities who are considered for positions. In decades past, before the civil rights movement took root, discrimination was more explicit. But the brazen injustices of yesterday have become the systemic disparities of today.

Expanding Our Horizons

We attended Lighthouse Gospel Chapel, which was recommended to us by Donovan Case, the father of my Kansas City roommate. The building was located at North Avenue and Thirty-fifth Street, right in the heart of Milwaukee's 'hood. The church ran a small community center that was the center of life in the area, providing food, clothing, recreation, and spiritual training for the families and youth of the area.

Lighthouse's pastor, James Carrington, had been saved off of the streets as a young man and eventually went on to Dallas Theological Seminary, before planting a church in Milwaukee. His commitment to Milwaukee's inner city has made him a respected and influential spiritual leader throughout the community.

At Lighthouse Gospel Chapel, Anitra and I got involved with the missions committee and helped Pastor Carrington organize various conferences and events. We knew we wanted to make a positive difference in the lives of people in urban Milwaukee, so becoming a part of Lighthouse was a great way to expand our ministry horizons.

Soul Food and Sushi

Throughout all of this change—a new city, new job, new wife, new church—I pressed forward to complete my master's degree at Marquette. Looking back, I marvel at the myriad responsibilities and pressures Anitra and I faced during that period. Clearly, God was supporting us through some very high-stress times.

As I neared completion of my master's and my GE training, I began to experience those familiar restless feelings about the future again. Would I continue in corporate America and seek advancement at GE? Would Anitra and I sell all of our stuff and head off to the mission field? Or was there something else for us altogether?

In addition to the Milwaukee area, GE had medical divisions in France and Japan. At one point, we had a team of Japanese engineers come to Waukesha, Wisconsin, to work on a project. Since I'm part Asian, I was eager to connect with them. I even took a class at Marquette to learn conversational Japanese, because it came into my head that Japan might be a country where we could settle as tentmaker missionaries.

Anitra and I befriended several members of the Japanese crew of engineers. We had them over for soul food (fried chicken and greens), and they had us over for sushi. And one team member, Nobuhiro Yoshizawa, tried to help me with my Japanese, while I tried helping him with his English. I even called my mom a couple times a week to practice my Japanese, since I knew that Momma had been forced to learn the language during Japan's occupation of Korea when she was a girl.

Just when I thought Japan or some other mission field would be our destiny after Milwaukee, we discovered something that sent all of our plotting and planning into a tailspin.

In 1993, Anitra announced she was pregnant. I was thrilled, and a bit frightened. I knew that raising a child would require everything we had, and we were already stretched pretty thin. Still, we rejoiced over the good news and thanked God for giving us a baby. As we started dreaming and preparing for the arrival of our newest family member, we both realized that the mission field—at least one in another country—would have to wait.

I began thinking in terms of continuing at GE beyond my master's degree and the Edison program. But the more I thought about it, the less enthusiastic I became.

As I looked at the other employees in the Edison program, I realized there were some who were on the career fast track and others who weren't. And once again, those who had the privileged pedigree and connections—and who were most likely playing golf with management—were the ones who got ahead fastest. Call me naïve, but before coming to GE, I had been totally oblivious to this reality.

GE hosted monthly African American forums, where various black employees gathered to discuss diversity and self-help issues in the company. During one of those events, I received an entirely new perspective on the value the business world places on social relationships outside the workplace.

It hit me like a nine iron. A guest speaker, Anthony Coleman, was addressing the forum one afternoon, and he flashed a slide on the screen that I'll always remember. The slide said: *Golf is the lan-*

guage of business. Coleman went on to explain why it was so important to learn how to play golf. He said countless major decisions related to job advancement and business deals take place on the eighteenth hole of a golf course. Soon after that, I took up golf (though I haven't progressed much since then). Those were the days before Tiger Woods hit the scene, so there wasn't a very visible role model in the PGA back then for young people. But now, young people—and especially young people of color—are being exposed to the game of golf like never before, and this is good. To this day, I encourage parents to enroll their children in golf classes, in addition to the standard piano, ballet, and karate lessons. I certainly planned to sign up our little boy (or girl) as soon as he was old enough.

Searching for a Heartbeat

I was certain our little baby was going to be a boy, even though we didn't want the doctor to tell us. I convinced Anitra that "Caleb" would be the perfect name. I imagined reading the Old Testament story of the twelve spies to him, showing him his name in the text, and then telling him that he (along with Joshua) was one of the brave spies who had faith that God would deliver Canaan to the Hebrew children. Caleb knew his God was greater than the big, bad giants that stood in the way of their "promised land." I could picture my little boy's smile growing wider as he discovered he was a hero in the Bible.

When Anitra and I went in for her prenatal checkup at seventeen weeks, her doctor had a concerned look. She called a couple nurses in to assist her, and they calmly but deliberately hooked up various gadgets to Anitra's belly. Finally, the doctor informed her that she couldn't find the baby's heartbeat.

During an earlier appointment, Anitra had taken an alpha feta protein test that indicated some signs of abnormality. The doctor speculated that the baby could have Down Syndrome or something worse and asked if we wanted to terminate the pregnancy.

Absolutely not, we told her. We wanted to have our baby. But now, they couldn't find a heartbeat. Anitra and I were both in shock. In fact, I didn't believe them. I wanted a second opinion, so we went to another doctor. But the result was the same; he couldn't find the heartbeat either. The only thing that kept me from completely losing myself in despair was knowing I had to stay strong for Anitra. I hugged her as we both cried.

It was one of the saddest days of our lives.

The doctors decided they needed to deliver the baby as soon as pos-sible, before complications arose with Anitra's health. They induced labor, and for more than ten hours Anitra toiled in the delivery room. I stood by her the whole time, holding her hand through the painful contractions, encouraging her the best I could. "Keep pushing, honey. I love you."

Finally our baby arrived, stillborn. It was a girl.

The doctors had warned us earlier that our baby's body might show signs of swelling and deterioration, since they were not sure when she had passed away. So we knew it would be difficult to see her.

Exhausted and overwhelmed by grief, Anitra didn't want her last memories of our baby to be any more upsetting, so she was afraid to hold her when the nurse presented the body to us. I gently stroked Anitra's sweat-beaded brow and said, "It's okay, honey."

So I held our little daughter for both of us. We named her Caleh.

For me, the hardest part was seeing my wife leave the hospital in a wheelchair without her baby, after having spent so many hours in labor. It was a defining moment for our marriage. Our grief brought us closer together in ways we didn't expect and would never want to repeat. We learned you couldn't take anything in life for granted. Nothing is promised. We learned that our faith in God was not just an intellectual concept; it became crucial to our survival. We learned that God's love for us, and our love for each other, could carry us through the most unbearable heartache.

In the weeks to follow, we discovered that many others around us had endured the pain and sorrow of losing a baby. People whom we would've never expected shared their stories of loss. It didn't make it easier, but it was heartening to know we were not alone.

A year later, on February 21, 1994, our sadness was eased by the joyous birth of our son, John. He was healthy and active, and he emerged with a head full of hair. After Anitra and I held him, the nurse cleaned him up, washed his head, and wrapped him in one of those blue-and-pink-striped baby blankets. And then the nurse, who was white, began picking out his hair like an Afro.

I laughed and said, "That's okay, you can just comb it." With a quarter Korean blood flowing through him, it was possible John would never have hair with the texture of an Afro. We were just happy to have a thriving little child to take home.

How to Control Your Destiny

At the end of 1994, I was a software systems engineer in the Magnetic Resonance Imaging Division at GE Medical Systems. The Edison program had stretched me in ways I'd never imagined, but it challenged me to be a better, smarter engineer. My knowledge of programming and software development grew exponentially. But more important, I gained greater insight into the value of leadership and interpersonal relationships in a corporate environment.

I would graduate from Marquette in May of 1995. With both the GE program and my master's courses winding down, I would soon be at a crossroads regarding my future. Anitra and I prayed and sought God's guidance, but I was not sure which direction He would take us.

Being in the Edison Engineering program afforded me the opportunity to hear Jack Welch speak at one of our corporate training programs. Welch was the illustrious chairman and CEO of General Electric from 1981 to 2001. He is credited with reinvigorating the company through his innovative leadership style, and transforming the face of American business in the process. His legend reverberated throughout the GE empire. His pithy, thought-provoking maxims were quoted throughout the business world:

"Change before you have to."

"Face reality as it is, not as it was or as you wish it to be."
"Mistakes can often be as good a teacher as success."

After hearing Welch speak live, my interest was piqued. Wanting to learn as much as I could about Welch and his leadership style, I picked up a 1993 book about Welch. The title was taken from another one of Welch's memorable quotes: *Control Your Own Destiny or Someone Else Will.*

The message of that title seized my attention. I didn't realize it then, but "control your own destiny" was what I had done when I decided to leave AlliedSignal, except my idea of controlling my destiny also involved handing over the reins to God. Now I was at a crossroads again. Which way would God direct?

With a small baby at home, I felt compelled to put the foreign missions dream on the shelf—at least for now. Some people at GE were driving south to Chicago to pursue MBAs at Northwestern and the University of Chicago on the weekends while still working in Waukesha. Was that a route for me? I considered this, but my vocational passion lay more with programming and software engineering than business and management.

Though I appreciated the opportunity I'd been given at GE, I had to accept the fact that at such a massive corporation I was basically a number, a labor statistic. Any drone could fill the job I was performing. I knew I was called to something more. And since it didn't appear I was on the fast track for advancement, like some others in the Edison program, I realized that GE held nothing for me in the long term.

Finally, I spoke with my faculty adviser at Marquette, Dr. James Heinen. He said, "Well, Andrew, why don't you apply for our Ph.D. program? You could take classes, do your course work, and then take a year off to write your dissertation."

I was taken aback. No one had ever suggested I pursue a doctoral program before. Actually, my brother Morgan, the aerospace engineer, might've mentioned it once when he was giving me a pep talk, but I wasn't really listening back then. Other than that, no one had seriously encouraged me to go the Ph.D. route.

Suddenly, my confidence was fired up. *Yeah, why not?* I thought to myself. I now knew I was capable of doing the work. Why shouldn't I pursue my doctorate?

Dr. Heinen provided me with that little nudge that we all need sometimes. It showed me the power of words and encouragement and high expectations. Because a college adviser thought I could do it, it made me think that maybe I could. In fact, I became confident that I would.

When I told Anitra, she was all for it. But she had one request. "Andrew," she said, "with a baby, a tight budget, and a husband who will need to spend a lot of time buried in his studies, this is going to be a challenge for me. I can do it, but I'd really like to be closer to family."

I totally understood. She was absolutely correct. Our young family would benefit immensely from the love, support, and free babysitting that only family and close friends could provide. Together, we prayed that God would make a way for us to go home.

The next day I called Florence Boldridge, the director of the minority engineering program at the University of Kansas. She was excited to hear I was interested in returning to KU. She spoke to Dean Carl Locke and Associate Dean Thomas Mulinazzi, from KU's engineering school, and arranged for me to fly down for a face-to-face meeting.

The meeting took place in March of 1995, about two months before my graduation from Marquette. Dean Mulinazzi's office walls were adorned with plaques and framed clippings representing various honors bestowed upon the KU engineering school. He sat behind a large oak desk, and as I settled into my seat, I could feel my heart rate rising.

"Andrew, we want you to come back to KU for your Ph.D.," he said matter-of-factly. "Just tell us what you'll need to make it happen. What do you need?"

Suddenly, I fancied myself a star point guard in an NBA owner's office, negotiating my next big contract to play for his team. I figured it was the closest I'd ever get to experiencing that feeling.

Jack Welch's famous quote flashed through my mind again: "Control your own destiny or someone else will." Sitting there, I quietly—and quickly—asked God to help me ask for the right things; to not be greedy, but to not be timid either.

I nervously told him the things I would need in terms of tuition, living arrangements, and money. Without missing a beat, he said, "Okay, you've got it. What else do you need?"

Once again, I realized that God was taking care of us. He would be faithful to strongly support Anitra, John, and me.

I was reminded of a maxim that Pastor Barbee would often recite: "Where God guides, He provides."

CHAPTER 11

The Making
of a Tentmaker

A s I write this, the first truly viable African American candidate for president is out on the campaign trail. Sometimes it's distressing to think that cultural milestones such as the ones I mentioned have taken so long reach. Though I'm encouraged that progress has been made, I know that there is much more to be done—especially in the sciences.

When I received my Ph.D. in 1999, I became the first African American to earn a doctorate in engineering from the University of Kansas. The first ever.

In the days leading up to the graduation ceremony, I thought about this often. How could it be? Why were there not more African Americans pursuing careers and advanced degrees in the engineering sciences?

Back then, I knew there were still plenty of black "firsts" yet to be conquered in the United States. Those were the days before Colin Powell's and Condoleezza Rice's respective appointments as secretaries of state; we were more than two years away from Halle

Berry becoming the first African American woman to win an Academy Award for Best Actress; and the cele-bration of the first African American football coach to lead his team to a Super Bowl victory (my friend and role model Tony Dungy) was still at least five years away.

As I write this, the first truly viable African American candidate for president is out on the campaign trail. Sometimes it's distressing to think that cultural milestones such as the ones I mentioned have taken so long to reach. Though I'm encouraged that progress has been made, I know that there is much more to be done—especially in the sciences.

I knew that one of the chief reasons why the leaders of KU's engineering school wanted me as a Ph.D. student was because they had no African American professors on their faculty. They hoped to groom me for such a role. When I first arrived at KU as a freshman in 1983, an African American engineering scholar named Dr. Bill Hogan served as the university's vice chancellor. He eventually left to become a CEO in corporate America, but not before becoming one of my engineering mentors. To this day, I call him up for advice and encouragement.

Because of my own journey, I understand the profound influence that role models like Dr Bill Hogan can have on the life of a young African American student. I've experienced it. And I used this knowledge as motivation for finishing my Ph.D. and making myself available to God for however He wanted to use me.

As I assisted students in the lab and taught undergrad classes, I began to catch a vision for how God could use my knowledge in electrical engineering and computer science to teach and inspire students, especially those from minority groups that were underrepresented in the fields of science, technology, engineering, and mathematics. In my heart, I sensed that He was preparing me for something special, and this motivated me to earn my Ph.D. quickly—not just for the sake of academic prestige or career advancement, but as a way of mentoring and inspiring tomorrow's generations of scientists and engineers.

God's Idea

When you pursue a Ph.D., it typically has to be based upon a fresh and novel angle on your field of study that no one else has covered. You, in effect, become the world's top expert on that particular slice of academic scholarship.

Initially, I was extremely nervous about coming up with something original enough to satisfy my Ph.D. advisers, Dr. Costas Tsatsoulis. I sweated and obsessed over what on earth I could propose that no one else had considered. But then God answered my prayer.

Thanks in part to my dad's influence, one of my historical role models was George Washington Carver. As a young student, I read about how Carver would go out to a field or garden and pray, asking God to show him things about His Creation. I decided to take a similar approach in the pursuit of my doctorate.

My first step was to acknowledge that all of science and creation belongs to God, and that if I had just one microscopic speck of His infinite knowledge, it would be enough to earn me a million Ph.D.s. So I said, "Lord, all I need is just enough to get one." Then I asked Him to show me what He wanted me to study for the next few years. "God," I implored, "please give me that one idea I'll need to earn my Ph.D." And He gave me an idea.

I decided to study the learning of interpersonal communication between different agents of artificial intelligence. If you have a group of intelligent agents (e.g., robots) that have different ways of conceptualizing what they know about the world, how can they communicate with each other if they don't share a common ontology or system of existence? My idea was that they do it by teaching each other what they mean by specific terms and words. Instead of sharing a common ontology, they learn to share a common distributive collective of memory. I applied this to the realm of computer search engine software.

This was back in the early days of Internet search engines, before Google existed. The idea was that a person would create a type of ontology, or categorization, of what they browsed on the World

Wide Web through their bookmark hierarchies. I developed intelligent software agents that would learn the distinguishing features for each of the categories, or concepts, for their users. Then, the different software agents would share examples of these concepts with each other in order to determine when they were "talking" about the same or similar concepts.

Thankfully, my adviser approved my course of study, and I was off on a whirlwind adventure of hypothesis, implementation, evaluation, and writing, writing, writing. Indeed, I wrote more papers during that intensive four-year span than I'd written my entire academic life.

It was challenging but fun—in a different sort of way. When one earns his Ph.D., he learns more about himself and his personal limitations than he'd ever realized before. I've heard more than one person liken earning a Ph.D. to running a marathon. If you hope to cross the finish line, you must pace yourself and train your mind and body to endure for the long haul.

One of my personal acronyms that guided me was PHD², or PHD times PHD. The first PHD had to do with my work ethic required to get a PHD: P = Perseverance, H = Hard work, and D = Discipline. The second PHD acronym had to do with my moral ethic: P = Purity, H = Humility, and D = Devotion to God. I wanted to succeed both in my work and in my morals because I had witnessed too many people who would trade one at the expense of the other. I was determined not to join their ranks.

When I began the program, Anitra gave me four years to finish. "If you're not done by then," she said, "then we need to move on." I'm glad she did, because it helped me focus intently on the task before me, and not drift into that listless complacency that slows down some Ph.D. candidates. By God's grace, I was able to press on. Also, I promised that if my family ever suffered too much financially, I would be willing to put my Ph.D. on hold to make sure that Anitra and our children were taken care of. Thankfully, I didn't have to stop.

Remembering Momma

In late 1995, my brother Morgan and his wife, Marian, who lived in a suburb of Los Angeles, brought my parents up from southern California to my sister Jeanne's home in Sacramento for Thanksgiving. My other siblings and their families also traveled to Sacramento for the holiday. With a limited budget, a pregnant wife (Anitra was expecting our second child, Adrianna) and a small baby to tote around, we decided to spend both Thanksgiving and Christmas in Kansas City with Anitra's family.

After the Christmas break, my sister Jeannie called to tell me Momma had been feeling under the weather with flulike symptoms when she saw her. Hearing this made me regret not joining them for the holidays. I knew my parents were getting older and that we weren't guaranteed tomorrow, let alone another year.

"Maybe we should go see her," I suddenly said to Anitra. Momma hadn't seen her grandson John for a while, and it would be good to spend some time with her and Dad.

Anitra agreed, but I knew it would be hard to get the time off from school, since it was the start of a new semester. I prayed about it and got permission from my adviser to take a week off. With Anitra pregnant and John just a little guy, it made the trip west a bit of a strain. But we endured.

It was January 1996. When we got to California, Momma looked fine. She didn't appear sick at all, and she was thrilled to see us. She said, "Let's go to McDonald's!" When I was a kid, it was always a treat for us to go to McDonald's. Momma loved seeing the grins on our faces when she announced we were going to Mickey D's. So, it brought a flood of wonderful memories to accompany her there again.

My mom had always planted positive seeds of confidence within me. When I'd come home from college during my undergrad years she would say, "Andrew, I believe you're doing good. You're making all As." Or, she'd cheer, "Andrew, you be the preacher! You be the preacher!" She was always encouraging.

In a quiet moment during our visit, I asked Momma how she was feeling.

"I have little cold, but I feel good," she told me. "I'll be okay, Andrew." And I had no reason to doubt her.

We returned to Kansas exhausted but thankful for the time away. I had a lot of catching up to do in my research, so I hit the ground running when I returned to KU.

Three days later, my brother Morgan called in a distraught voice and said simply, "She's dead, Andrew. Mom's dead."

My precious Momma, who had suffered so much her entire life but still did her best to give my siblings and me a better childhood than her own, was gone at only sixty-two years of age.

I was devastated. Besides our late baby, Caleb, I had never lost anyone that close to me. I wept until I was too exhausted to weep anymore. All of us were at a loss, especially Dad. He mostly sat in silence, staring blankly into space. Though he and Momma sometimes had a rocky marriage, we could tell he missed her. He was hurting.

The family decided that Momma should be buried at Fort Riley in Kansas, close to our old Junction City home. At the memorial service, I read a short essay that I'd written as a tribute to Momma. It was called "A Birth of a Nation." I reflected on how she had come from another country to give all of us a loving home; how Dad had traveled back across the sea to get her, Robert, Jeanne, and Morgan; how both Momma and Dad had given so much for their children; how insignificant my mom's life must've seemed to some people because she wasn't educated and could hardly speak English. But then I expressed how special and how valued she was to me, and all the love and the sacrifice she gave for me.

I choked up and stumbled over my words several times as I read the essay, but was eventually able to finish amid my tears.

Right on Time

Three months after Momma's passing, in March of 1996, our second child, Adrianna, was born. We were thrilled to have a daughter, and I was thankful to see that she inherited her mom's looks.

Throughout my four years of Ph.D. study, God provided employment opportunities to supplement my work at KU. One summer, GE sponsored me for a GEM engineering fellowship that paid for a lot of my doctoral research. It required me to work at GE's Corporate Research and Development Center in Schenectady, New York. The following summer, Lucent Technologies hired me and allowed me to telecommute from Lawrence.

During various periods of my Ph.D. program, our family funds dwindled down to desperate levels. Feeding an increasing number of mouths and diapering multiple bottoms stretched our budget in ways I hadn't anticipated when I negotiated my terms with Dean Locke and Associate Dean Mulinazzi. Again, we prayed for faith and trusted in God's provision.

Soon my old friend Antoine Lawrence, who now worked as a Unix systems administrator at a firm in Kansas City, helped secure me a part-time job at his company. Though it was only about eighteen hours a week, it paid more than I had made at GE. Once again, God provided.

My Next Mission Field

My memories of these days are mostly a blur—lab work, teaching, research, part-time job, come home, repeat. Our days were full of nonstop activity; Anitra's schedule, which was equally demanding, was now mostly spent fulfilling her role as stay-at-home mom to John and Adrianna.

During my internship at GE in New York, Anitra had worked part-time at an airline reservation office in Lawrence while friends from our church took turns babysitting our kids. One afternoon there was a tornado in the Lawrence area while I was in New York, and Anitra had to pick up the kids, John and baby Adrianna, from the babysitter's house, drive home in the heavy rain, and hide out in the bathtub while the storm passed over. I prayed, and had the confidence that they were safely covered by God's protection. Nonetheless, days like that one made me strive to avoid being away from my Anitra and the kids for extended periods of time.

Despite all of our busyness, we managed to remain active with church ministry, too. It was good to be back at Victory Bible Church with Pastor Barbee, and Anitra and I enjoyed leading a weekly Bible study for young married couples.

As my Ph.D. completion date drew nearer, I also started interviewing for faculty positions. By now, I knew that God was calling me to teach on the college level. I would still be a tentmaker missionary, but now my mission field would be to young men and women on a university campus. I just needed to figure out where He wanted me to do it.

Anitra's mother continued her battle with multiple sclerosis, and Anitra felt uncomfortable moving too far away from her. So she and I decided that wherever we wound up, it should be within a day's drive of Kansas City.

I interviewed for a slot in the computer science department at Iowa State in Ames. Dr. Derrick Rollins, who had been mentored by Pastor Barbee before I arrived at KU, worked at Iowa State and was able to get me the opportunity and offer a strong recommendation. I also spoke to the engineering schools at the University of Missouri–Kansas City (Anitra's alma mater), the University of Nebraska in Lincoln, and the University of Kansas. Each school made an offer for a faculty position, except Nebraska, which made me an offer to help it start a student-operated Internet company in conjunction with their business school. These opportunities put me in the enviable bind of having to choose.

KU, of course, was my first choice. But the engineering school had recently experienced a change in leadership, and while the interim department chair did eventually extend an offer, I could tell there was a little hesitancy. I took it as a sign that God was guiding me to not be too hasty in making my decision. While KU was my hands-down favorite, I sensed I needed to be more open to other possibilities as well. Derrick told me, "If you stay at KU, they're going to always think of you as a graduate student. You'll never be taken seriously as a scholar in your own right." Although KU would have been the most comfortable place to go, and they would've paid me quite handsomely, I was drawn to the adventure of a place like Iowa State, which had an great reputation as an engineering research institution. Iowa State was also where my role model George Washington Carver received his graduate degree and later became the school's first black faculty member.

Unfortunately, there wasn't as cohesive a relationship between the computer science and engineering departments at Iowa State, which could make the kind of research in which I was interested more difficult to undertake. While all of this was happening, somehow recruiters from the University of Iowa in Iowa City found out that Iowa State had made me an offer, and at the last minute they asked to interview me.

So I traveled to the University of Iowa for the interview and immediately liked the community. People in Iowa City bragged of a more cosmopolitan feel (if any city in the corn-rich state of Iowa could ever be considered cosmopolitan), and a sophisticated sense of scholarship and culture dominated the campus vibe. For sure, Iowa City did appear more urbane than Ames, which felt decidedly more agricultural in its ethos. I liked the fact that the University of Iowa's College of Engineering did lots of work with the College of Medicine and university hospital, which at that time was the second largest teaching-affiliated hospital in the country.

Still, Iowa State was an excellent institution—and their offer was nothing to sneeze at. Though we'd narrowed our choices down to two, we had a tough decision on our hands.

Together, Anitra and I once again sought God's direction. We sensed He was calling us to Iowa. But, the question was, *which* Iowa?

CHAPTER 12

Iowa Epiphanies

I accepted the offer from the University of Iowa. The next weekend, Anitra and I traveled to Iowa City and quickly found a house that we both loved. But before we could devote our full attention to moving, I had to complete my dissertation.

At times, I was not sure how I would make it to the finish line. I was burning the midnight oil, but I eventually got to a point where I had no more oil to burn. I reminded God of my earlier prayers (as if He needed reminding); I told Him there was no way I could complete my Ph.D. apart from His help.

On two separate occasions I was hit with stamina-draining cases of bronchitis that brought all my activities to a halt. The stress was beating me down, and I had no idea how to turn it off.

"You need to slow down and pace yourself better," Anitra counseled. "If you're not careful, you won't see your Ph.D. or your next birthday. And we need you alive, honey."

My wife was gracious, but I was a pain to live with back then, particularly the months after my mom died. Easily irritated, I was alternately angry, depressed, or ecstatic, depending on how well my research and writing had gone that day.

Adding to the drama of this period was Anitra's pregnancy with our third surviving child. Rosa Marie was born on February 21, 1999, five years to the day after John was born, and life immediately shot to another level of intensity. Still, amid my hectic pace of life, I rejoiced at the gift of another healthy, beautiful daughter. I remembered reading about the Rose of Sharon in the Bible, so Rosa's name was loosely tied to that of my former nursery school teacher, Sharon Scoggins. But Anitra and I also admired Rosa Parks as an icon of the civil rights movement. Either way, our Rosa was named for two strong, memorable women.

The spring of '99 marked the culmination of my Ph.D. journey. Though it had been a hard road, with the support of Anitra and other friends and mentors, I persevered and finished the dissertation. The written portion numbered a few hundred pages. By the end, I knew that I had given the project all I had.

Defending my work before the dissertation committee was nerve-racking. Because my Ph.D. adviser, Dr. Costas Tsatsoulis, had traveled out of the country during the end stretch of my research and writing, my final dissertation was not as polished or cohesive as it could have been had he been more accessible. This wasn't Professor Tsatsoulis's fault, though. I could have waited to present my dissertation later, but I was fearful of not completing the process before I left KU and becoming, instead of a Ph.D., one of those perpetual "ABDs" (All-But-the-Dissertation). Consequently, there were a few loose ends, and the probing questions from the committee exposed some of my dissertation's weaknesses.

Despite my anxiety, however, the members of the committee were able to see the quality of my research and the extraordinary amount of effort I had poured into it. They asked me to correct a few problem areas and redo those sections of my presentation, but overall they were very pleased.

By God's grace, I passed! I was now ready, at least on paper, to greet the world as Dr. Andrew Williams.

Welcome to Iowa City

We moved to Iowa City that summer. Now with three young children in tow in our tiny, white Honda Civic hatchback, it wasn't an easy task. But we were buoyed by the excitement of beginning a new chapter of our lives.

I was especially eager to finally put all of my education and training—from undergrad to AlliedSignal to General Electric to grad school to my Ph.D.—to work in a place where I could teach and mentor fledgling engineers and computer scientists. I was humbled to think that I could instruct and inspire young minds in the same way that I had been taught and mentored by so many others. I was now able to give back in earnest.

Most of all, I hoped to be able to do my job in a way that would reflect my values and faith. The UI campus would become my first official chance to be the tentmaker missionary that I had been itching to become.

Iowa City was a relatively small town—about 62,000 including the student population—so there were a limited number of African American or cross-cultural churches. But after a few stops at other churches, we finally settled at Bethel AME, a tiny African Methodist Episcopal church that was built outside the city limits in 1868, back when blacks could not own property in the city.

The first time we walked into the church building, we thought we were in the foyer—but it was *the church*. The small frame building was one of Iowa City's oldest structures, and its only historically black church. The congregation only had twenty-five or thirty members, but it was a friendly group of mostly older believers who truly loved God.

Since there weren't that many opportunities for youth or college-age ministry at Bethel, I connected with other local churches and ministries. I met Jesse Bradley, the white youth pastor at Park View Evangelical Free Church, which had a thriving college ministry. We bonded quickly, especially after we discovered a mutual acquaintance. While Jesse was a student at Dallas Theological Seminary, he had attended Concord Baptist Church in Dallas, where my dear friend Leroy Armstrong was an assistant pastor. We shared the common bond of having had Leroy as a friend.

At Concord Baptist, Jesse had been one of the few whites in a predominantly African American congregation. He had a heart for urban ministry and for breaking down the walls of racial separation in the church. I sensed in him a kindred spirit, so I talked to him about helping him out with ministry to the African American students at UI.

Jesse and I prayed for UI's black students, who sometimes seemed isolated or marginalized from the majority community. We spent time discussing the best approaches for reaching out to them. Finally, we prayed to God that if He really wanted us to do this, He would send us some passionate student leaders who could give us "street cred" and become our link to the student population.

God answered our prayer in the form of a junior named Dara. She was an education major and a committed Christian who hungered for a more vibrant spiritual community on the UI campus. Jesse also introduced me to Tony Gatewood, a freshman from the projects on the south side of Chicago. With the help of Dara and Tony, Jesse and I launched a ministry to black students called Harambee (a tribute to the memory of the student ministry that had changed my life at KU). We gathered together weekly for Bible study, prayer, singing, and conversation about the real-life concerns facing students on the campus. On any given week, we discussed topics as diverse as time management, sex outside of marriage, and racism.

We began with only a handful of students and our group only grew slightly, but I remember from the small group of students at KU's Harambee that it was not the numbers that counted but rather the amount of impact a person could have on individual lives. All I had to do was look at my own life to see how previous mentors and spiritual leaders had helped me when I didn't have much to offer.

Jesse was gracious to let me help with leadership of the group, even though I was not a member of his church, and I would occasionally deliver a devotional message. It was a wonderful opportunity to share my faith, and I relished every minute of it.

I was transported back to a fateful day during my sophomore year at KU, when Mike Jordahl asked me to share my testimony during an outdoor evangelistic event sponsored by the Navigators. At first I was reluctant. It was outside on the campus grounds where all manner of folks were passing by. But as God's Spirit moved, I became more confident and bold. I remembered those days from fifth grade when I had earned the nickname of "Elijah" because of my frequent testifying. I realized how God was preparing me even then for the ministry He would give me two decades later.

I remembered the training and encouragement I had received from Pastor Barbee's, Pastor Briscoe's, and Pastor Carrington's churches, how they had each asked me to preach from the pulpit. Each time, I had approached the platform with fear and trembling, but each time I ended up rejoicing as I witnessed God's Spirit moving through my imperfect words.

Now I was witnessing God work in the lives of young students who might one day be mentoring other students, and the legacy goes on and on. I marveled at God's brilliant design and recommitted myself to faithfully pursuing my call to "advertise God's glory" to the world. I had no idea then that I would one day see fruit from those efforts when my path crossed with Tony Gatewood's a few years later.

Scientific Breakthroughs

Earning my Ph.D. prepared me well for the nonstop "research mode" expected from engineering professors at a major research institution like the University of Iowa. I was fortunate to connect with an excellent research mentor in the Engineering and Computer Science department, Professor Tom Casavant. He would meet with me regularly to discuss ideas and help me figure out how to write effective proposals for research grants.

Tom also introduced me to Dr. Ed Stone, a researcher in the

medical school and one of Tom's research collaborators. Ed, who received $1 million a year from the Howard Hughes Medical Institute for his groundbreaking work, specialized in ophthalmology and genetics. My idea of getting intelligent software agents with diverse ontologies to communicate and learn from each other actually applied to a problem that Ed described involving clinicians trying to define new disease subtypes related to the genetic origins of eye diseases that cause blindness. I'm sure that sounds a bit convoluted to laymen's ears, but it brought amazing clarity to my research. Remarkably, I was able to transfer some of the principles Ed used to identify eye diseases to my artificial intelligence (AI) work. Finally, some of the mental obstacles that had hindered my ability to articulate my hypothesis were stripped away and made relatable to the concepts gleaned from Ed's genome research. My vision for AI suddenly had a more practical and meaningful purpose as I applied its concepts to the world of genomic medicine. Once again, I witnessed God connecting me with the people and ideas I needed to know at the exact time when I needed them.

Tom and Ed guided me in writing a proposal for the National Institutes of Health (NIH). And after an enormous effort that required many late nights, I submitted the plan. Then, I prayed.

Regardless of the outcome, I felt I was in my element vocationally. My experience with GE Medical Systems had given me a taste of working in the field of medical technology. Now, working at a university with a world-class medical school exposed me to another side of the process. I could now better connect the dots between the machines we were making at GE and the ways they could be used by physicians and scientists to further our understanding of medicine. At AlliedSignal, my engineering skills had helped build the nonnuclear components of nuclear weapons. But at GE, I had helped build devices that heal. I embraced the chance to do more of that at Iowa.

My proposal was rejected twice before finally being accepted, which reminded me about the importance of persistence in science. I won a three-year $770,000 grant from the National Eye Institute that allowed me to delve deeper into my research. With the money,

I was able to hire graduate students and a postdoctoral researcher to assist me with my work, as well as collaborate with key experts at research universities around the world and take advantage of their knowledge.

Even as I experienced professional success, I received occasional reminders of the disheartening aspects of being an African American academician at a predominantly white university. One day, for reasons I can no longer recall, a white colleague began talking to me about affirmative action in higher education. I always cringed whenever the conversations at work turned to race or politics, and this time was no exception.

"Andrew, you're black," the faculty member said. "You'll get tenure for sure."

He went on to talk about a woman who had previously worked in the college of engineering before leaving for another research university on the West Coast, where she quickly received tenure. "It was easy for her to get tenure there because she's a woman," he said.

It was neither the first nor the last time that I heard comments such as these. I knew these attitudes existed; I just hoped they didn't exist in someone who had a voice in determining my future. Though he didn't recognize it, my colleague's words revealed a latent prejudice that grouped all minorities in a box that says, "You're not here because you're smart or talented, but because your kind is underrepresented." While I knew this wasn't true, I realized it was something that most minority students and professionals would have to encounter sooner or later. I actually felt the opposite. I had seen many blacks who felt that they had to be twice as good as another person in order to achieve success in a world where they often began at a social and economic disadvantage. In reality, affirmative action had long existed for those in the majority race and gender.

Purpose-Driven Revelations

Two key experiences began to transform my vision for work and ministry in ways that would have long-lasting implications.

The first experience was related to robots. In addition to my grant from the NIH, I was also getting funding from Microsoft, with whom I had established a friendly relationship. Soon after arriving at UI, I met with a Microsoft representative about some of the ideas I had to help expose more racial minorities and women to science, mathematics, and technology. When they contacted me a few weeks later expressing a desire to help, I knew it was God's favor.

One of my ideas was to launch a weekend day camp for middle school–age boys and girls from minority communities that were underrepresented in the fields of science and technology. I chose that age because it was when I had first become interested in programming computers and video games. I wanted those kids to get hands-on experience working with computers and technology, the same way I did when my brother Morgan had let me play that old *Star Trek* game in the KU computer lab some twenty-five years earlier.

Our Electrical Engineering department and College of Engineering were very supportive. We attracted six kids the first year and about fifteen the next (the program has grown even more since then, but more on that later). My hope was to plant within each of those young people a desire for learning and knowledge, and a sense that they belonged in a college environment just as much as anyone else.

Part of the day-camp experience involved programming and playing with four-legged Sony AIBO robots. In fact, interacting with those mechanical mutts quickly became the highlight of the weekend for many of the kids. They loved "teaching" the robots to walk, sit, and stand on their hind legs. It was a great way to show kids how fun science can be.

I initially saw the AIBOs used in the popular RoboCup soccer events that allowed computer-engineering students to flex their programming skills in a competitive setting. But my first up-close encounter came in 2001 at the International Conference on Autonomous Agents in Montreal, Canada. When I watched the things engineers were doing with the AIBOs, I got chills. Though they were designed to look like cute puppies, these little creatures were on the cutting edge of artificial intelligence. I knew then that I wanted to incorporate the AIBO robots into my curriculum—and perhaps, one day, lead a RoboCup team in international competition.

My second key experience was related to a book. In late 2003 I read California pastor Rick Warren's bestseller *The Purpose-Driven Life*. As I read, I was deeply affected by the powerful simplicity of Warren's words and his emphasis on the unique calling of each individual. "Your abilities were not given just to make a living; God gave them to you for your ministry," Warren wrote. And then this: "God will never ask you to dedicate your life to a task you have no talent for. On the other hand, the abilities you *do* have are a strong indication of what God wants you to do with your life. They are clues to knowing God's will for you."[2]

Warren employed an acrostic called S.H.A.P.E. to describe each person's unique calling and purpose. According to Warren, we are a composite of at least five different God-given factors:

Spiritual gifts

Heart

Abilities

Personality

Experience

In the weeks that followed, as I pondered Warren's words and thought about the gifts, passions, and encounters God had allowed me to have, I experienced an epiphany of sorts. One morning while having my quiet time and writing in my journal, I was inspired to craft my own purpose statement. I ignored the sounds of my children beginning to wake up and play with their toys, so I could quickly jot down my thoughts. I needed to embrace the muse while it was near.

Like Warren, I also decided to make use of an acrostic, but mine would be related to something I did every day when I got to work. I began scribbling, "My mission in life, both personal and professional, is to T.E.A.C.H.:

Teach to encourage the body of Christ

Enable young African Americans to reach their full potential spiritually, academically, vocationally, and economically

Advertise the glory of God and the gospel

Create community and

Humbly learn from Christ

The words rushed through my heart and mind and out of my pen like a surge of electricity. When I finished, I knew without a doubt that something was about to change. God was stirring again.

Later that day, I looked at the students in my class. It was exactly like all of my other classes—a roomful of white males, with one or two white females sprinkled in here and there and an occasional Asian American male. There were no African Americans. While I cared deeply for all of my students, regardless of race, and knew for a fact that God had entrusted them in my care, I suspected there was something more. *If God wants me to help young African American men and women,* I thought to myself, *is this the place where He's calling me to do it?*

I was in my fifth year at UI, and in that period I had only taught two African American students and one African student. And some of my classes had been as large as fifty or sixty students. Part of it, I understood, was that we were in Middle America, out in the center of cornfields—not too many black students were drawn to that environment.

But an even larger factor, sadly, was that the numbers of African American students who pursue careers in science, technology, engineering, and mathematics were depressingly low nationwide. I knew that one reason for this was the high attrition rates among

African American college students. Statistics reveal that in 2001 African American students made up 13.3 percent of incoming college freshmen, but four years later they only received 9 percent of the bachelor's degrees—and a measly 8 percent of the degrees in science and technology majors.

Comparatively, during that same period, white students comprised 74.8 percent of incoming freshmen and later earned 70.2 percent of all bachelor's degrees, including 67.3 percent of the degrees granted in the science and technology majors.[3]

I realized that another factor in the disparity of black students successfully making it through college—and majoring in the fields of science and technology—is the lack of African American role models on the college and university level. There are simply not enough black engineering professors, and this has devastating consequences beyond the simple lack of diversity on college campuses. It subconsciously sends a disheartening message to African American college students who are still at a formative stage in their lives. They need to see that careers in science, technology, and mathematics are a possibility for them.

This is one reason why I felt compelled to rethink my presence at a school like the University of Iowa. I sensed that my purpose statement might be better pursued in a more diverse setting. But where? What's more, after five years in Iowa City, and with three young children, would Anitra be ready to pull up the stakes for another major move?

I prayed for God's wisdom. I prayed not knowing where we would be led next, but certain that it would be a place where T.E.A.C.H. could become my daily reality.

CHAPTER 13

The SpelBots Cometh

All along the way, I shared with Anitra the revelations I'd been having at work and in my spiritual life. We prayed together daily for God's direction. She knew how enthralled I'd been by the message of *The Purpose-Driven Life* and how determined I was to make a difference in the lives of minority students. So she wasn't at all surprised when I broached the topic of leaving Iowa City.

"Andrew, if God is leading you to another school, I support it," she said. "I knew that Iowa was not the end of our journey."

I looked into her eyes and fell in love all over again, this woman who had always stood by me, even when I had no idea what I was doing. I kissed her and whispered, "I love you forever." It was a relief to know that my wife and best friend was on my side.

With that, the search was on.

I knew that geography would make a big difference in the number of African American students enrolled at prospective schools. A state university in Charlotte, Chicago, or Houston would almost certainly be more racially diverse than UI. Still, I never considered pursuing jobs at other big state schools. It occurred to me that this could be my chance to explore working at a Historically Black College and University (HBCU).

In fact, when I thought about it, working at an HBCU had been one of my life dreams ever since my dad turned me on to what George Washington Carver had done at Tuskegee Institute, but I always thought I would wait until my retirement years to work at one. I had never considered leaving a major research university in the prime of my academic career for an HBCU. But then I thought to myself, *If you're really called to reach African American students, why not seek a position at a Historically Black College and University while you can offer the best years of your life?*

Why not, indeed.

HBCUs are comprised of 110 public and private African American schools of higher education—colleges, junior colleges, universities, seminaries, and medical schools—that were founded prior to 1964. Legendary institutions such as Tuskegee University in Alabama, Hampton University in Virginia, and Florida A&M all belong to the HBCU family. Famous and influential names like Thurgood Marshall, Alex Haley, Toni Morrison, and Oprah Winfrey are among countless HBCU alumni.

All my life, I'd been a part of mostly white or multiracial institutions—my jobs, my schools, my places of worship. Even when I did join a predominantly black church like Paseo Baptist or Lighthouse Gospel Chapel, there were other—*whiter*—parts of my life that balanced it out. But to actually work somewhere that was black-owned and operated? What would that feel like? Would I feel out of place? Would I make enough money to survive? Could I handle the change from big-white-school politics to smaller-black-school politics? Would I be cheating myself personally or professionally? These are all questions that ran through my head as I began to seriously put the possibility of teaching at an HBCU on the table.

Checking out the ads in the *Communications of the ACM* (the official magazine of the Association for Computing Machinery, the professional organization for computer scientists), I discovered an electrical and computer engineering faculty position opening at Howard University that caught my attention. Located in the nation's capital, Howard has a reputation as a vigorous research institution that reportedly produces more African American Ph.D.s than any other university in the world. I contacted them and flew to D.C. for an interview. The school occupied an urban campus not far from the bustle of downtown Washington. It was quite a contrast to the more far-flung locales of Iowa and Kansas.

After touring the campus and interviewing with the department chair, the electrical and computer engineering faculty, and several computer science students, I had a good feeling about Howard. I was also drawn to the notion of being based in a truly cosmopolitan city like Washington, within easy reach of some of the nation's best science museums and research institutions. The interviews went well, and I felt it was a place where I could thrive. But the search was just beginning.

Georgia on Our Minds

In 2004 my old Navigators friend and mentor, Mike Jordahl, was on the verge of becoming a national director of the Collegiate Navigators. When he heard I might be looking for positions at HBCUs, he connected me with Rich Berry, the national director of the Navigators' African American ministries. Rich and I had a nice chat on the phone. He told me about some of the outreach ministries he had to African Americans in his home base of Atlanta. "Why don't you come down and check us out?" he said. "We've got a lot of good stuff going on down here."

Anitra and I had been to "Hotlanta" together before. Back during my grad school days at KU, Anitra had won a free trip for two. We secured a babysitter and took off for a brief vacation. We both loved the city and said at the time that we'd like to visit again, so it didn't require much work for Rich to persuade me to come. Anitra and I did the four-hour drive to Kansas City to drop the kids off with their Uncle George and Aunt Trudy (who had moved back to the Kansas area from California when George changed jobs), and then we flew down to Georgia for a whirlwind visit.

Rich and his wife, Jane, showed us around town, introduced us to some of their friends, and took us out to eat. Atlanta was just as colorful and dynamic as we remembered. It was exciting to see so many nice African American neighborhoods, populated by successful black professionals. The number of flourishing, black-owned businesses was inspiring as well. In some ways, it was like an alternate universe to what we'd seen in places like Milwaukee and Iowa City. We were reminded that there is indeed a thriving African American middle class with an abundance of positive role models.

Atlanta was also rich in HBCUs. The Atlanta University Center, located on the city's southwest side, is a consortium of five historically black schools, including Clark Atlanta University, Morehouse College, Spelman College, the Interdenominational Theological Center, and the Morehouse School of Medicine. The schools share a library and allow their students to cross-register for classes and programs within the consortium. To my mind, having so many historic black colleges clustered together seemed akin to visiting the Boston area and being in proximity of Harvard, MIT, and the New England Conservatory, among many others. In addition to the HBCUs, Atlanta was also home to strong institutions like Georgia Tech and Emory University. For both student and scholar, Atlanta was a kind of southern mecca of higher education.

"Since we're down here," I told Rich, "I'd love to connect with the computer science departments at Morehouse and Spelman, just to see what they're like." I had heard a lot about the special connection between Spelman, a women's college, and Morehouse, a men's school. I was curious to see how they worked together.

Before leaving for Atlanta, I had visited Spelman's Web site and found the e-mail address of the department chair at Spelman. She told me she would be in and that I should drop by. "We're going to have some openings in the fall," she informed me after we arrived on the campus. She encouraged me to apply, which I wasted no time in doing.

Rich also introduced me to a friend who was a vice president at Morehouse College. In turn, he was able to arrange a meeting for me with the dean at Morehouse, which is literally across the street from Spelman. I met with him later that same day and talked about the possibility of working at Morehouse. All in all, it was a productive trip.

When Anitra and I returned to Iowa, we learned that Howard University wanted to make me an offer. While we were pleased to hear this, we were both starting to get excited about the possibility of moving to Atlanta. We loved the culture, the vitality, and the weather—well, at least when compared to the Iowa and Wisconsin winters.

Then, months later, Spelman flew me back to Atlanta for an interview with Provost Dr. Sharon Washington and several faculty members and students from the Computer and Information Sciences Department. Soon, I would have an offer from Spelman, but waited on an official offer from Howard.

Though Anitra and I preferred Atlanta to Washington, D.C., we wanted to remain open to where God might be leading us. So we continued to pray.

"You mean, you wouldn't mind me teaching at an all-women's college?" I said to Anitra.

"Don't you want *our* daughters to have the best faculty, male or female, to teach them when they go to college?" she said.

I nodded my head. "Of course."

"Then you should be willing to teach at Spelman."

Anitra was right, but I did wonder about the prospect of being a male professor at a women's school. Was I prepared to be the only guy in the room? Would the students respect me as much as their female professors? I wasn't accustomed to working with so many women. Unfortunately, up to that time men had always dominated the engineering field and college technology departments.

Then I remembered my call to reach minority students, especially those who were underrepresented in the fields of science and technology. I thought about the dearth of African Americans in the sciences, and the even greater lack of female African Americans. And my wife's convicting words about our daughters made me think of Spelman students as the daughters of other men and women who wanted the best faculty to teach their kids as well.

When I interviewed at Spelman, I gave a talk to the computer science majors about my engineering background and some of the areas of technology that interested me most. I even brought along an older edition of the Sony AIBO to demonstrate how I'd want to incorporate robotics into my curriculum.

After I spoke, a junior named Aryen Moore-Alston approached me. Aryen (pronounced like Orion) was fascinated by the AIBO and artificial intelligence. She wanted to learn more. I also chatted with a junior named Brandy Kinlaw, whom it turns out I had met a year earlier at the Richard Tapia Celebration of Diversity in Computing Conference in Atlanta. We talked about the Lego Mindstorms Robot research project she had presented at the conference. Brandy showed me her small robot and portions of her presentation. It was exciting to see students already engrossed by the possibilities of robotics and artificial intelligence. The Spelman students were inquisitive and genuinely engaged. I liked that.

By this time, if it isn't obvious, I had a pretty good idea of what my choice would be. But before accepting Spelman's offer, I spoke to Provost Washington about the possibility of acquiring four AIBOs for the computer science department. I explained to her my dream of forming a robotics team that could one day compete in the International RoboCup. When she agreed to buy the robots, I knew the search was over.

We were going to Spelman College.

Atlanta Wellspring

I moved my family to Atlanta late in the summer of 2004: (Anitra's mother passed away before we moved.) We found a house and got settled in just in time for the fall semester. On my first day of courses, as I looked at the diverse assortment of young, intelligent

Spelman women and Morehouse men in my classrooms, I was overcome by a sense of purpose and excitement. And I was humbled by the conviction that, in this moment of my life, I was precisely where God wanted me to be.

I quickly became engrossed with Spelman's rich history as the nation's oldest historically black college for women. Like many of the other HBCUs, Spelman's origins were rooted in the Christian church. Originally called the Atlanta Baptist Female Seminary, it was founded in 1881 by two white female missionaries from Massachusetts. Visiting Atlanta, the women were so appalled by the impoverished conditions of the African American community that they determined to start a school that could educate black women for leadership. One of their biggest benefactors was the renowned oil magnate and philanthropist John D. Rockefeller, whose wife, Laura Spelman Rockefeller, was a great advocate of the seminary. In 1884, the name of the school was changed to honor Laura and her parents, who had been active in the antislavery movement. The school transitioned from a seminary to a college in 1924, and became officially affiliated with Morehouse College, as part of the Atlanta University Center, in 1929.

Today, the Spelman/Morehouse combo represents one of the most storied wellsprings of African American culture, having graduated such influential public figures as educator Marian Wright Edelman, novelist Alice Walker, civil rights champion Martin Luther King, Jr., and filmmaker Spike Lee. At times, I had to pause and soak in the magnitude of the place—the history of which I was now a part. Thinking of all that Spelman stands for, I prayed for the wisdom and courage to build upon, and not diminish, that great legacy.

Building a Team

Back in the summer, as I was preparing to make the move south to Spelman, Aryen Moore-Alston, whom I had met during my interview, called me in Iowa. She told me she was doing an internship in robotics at the NASA Jet Propulsion Laboratory in Pasadena, working with the noted robotics engineer Dr. Ayanna Howard (who also is African American). Aryen explained that she was using the AIBOs and asked if I could recommend any helpful books. I gave her a few suggestions, and then decided to prime the pump for the fall. With the great experience she was gaining from her internship, I suspected that getting Aryen on the robotics team would be quite a coup.

I said, "So, you must've heard that I'm coming to Spelman in the fall, right?"

But to my surprise she had not. She simply called because she'd remembered my AIBO talk during my Spelman interview, and now she needed more information. She was happy to hear that I would be coming, though. I told her I looked forward to seeing her in Atlanta.

That fall when I saw Aryen, who was now a senior, I wasted no time introducing her to the idea of a Spelman robotics team, painting a vivid picture of competing in the RoboCup soccer tournament in Osaka, Japan. That was coincidental since Aryen had spent a year in Japan while in Spelman's Study Abroad Program. However, she had no idea what I was talking about with RoboCup, so I showed her some video clips of the event. That sparked her interest a little, but I could tell she still wasn't completely sold. I knew that a Spelman RoboCup team didn't stand a chance without a strong student leader who could command the respect of her classmates, as well as become the public voice of the group.

"Aryen, I'd like you to consider becoming the captain of the team." Though she was a busy student, with an array of extracurricular interests, my enthusiastic pitch eventually won her over. I had my first recruit.

Next I targeted Brandy Kinlaw, also now a senior, whom I knew had superb programming skills, probably the best among Spelman's computer science majors. I had been so impressed with the Lego robot project from the Tapia conference that I asked her to become one of my student assistants for my continuing robotics research. My only condition was that she also join the new robotics team. I didn't have to twist her arm. She signed on and became the team's lead software integrator, which basically meant she led our programming efforts.

So I had my captain and my chief programmer.

Now, I set out to complete the roster. I told the students in my Data Structures and Algorithms class about the robotics team and invited anyone interested to join. Data Structures was my most advanced course that fall semester. It featured a class full of exceptionally bright computer science students, including eight Spelman students and twelve men from Morehouse. I didn't receive inquiries from any of the men, but one of my Spelman students—junior Ebony Smith—approached me after class to join the team. Shinese Noble, a senior, came to my office after that and asked if she could join the team. She had heard about the team from her friends.

Then, I invited two of my sophomore students, Ebony O'Neal and Karina Liles, to join. Both of them were assigned to me through NASA's Model Institutions for Excellence (MIE) Program, a national research internship project based in a select group of colleges and universities. The MIE Program provided scholarships and internship opportunities in an effort to increase student participation in science, engineering, and mathematics. Since a big part of my mission entails getting minority students more involved in the fields of science and technology, I was more than happy to serve as an MIE adviser at Spelman. Using my adviser clout, I strongly suggested that Ebony and Karina fulfill some of their MIE research through participation on the robotics team. They graciously concurred.

And then there were six.

Finally, the Spelman robotics team—or SpelBots, as I suggested we call ourselves during our first meeting—was a reality. What began as an ambitious dream was suddenly animated by the personality and intellect of six extraordinary young women.

I gave thanks to God, understanding that my hopes and aspirations were no longer my own. I now needed to gradually step out of the way and allow the SpelBots to take ownership of their destiny.

Unexpected Friends

During our first few meetings, it became painfully evident that we would have a lot of work to do to get up to speed on using the AIBOs. I shared with the students my vision for what we were trying to do, went over the rules of RoboCup competition, and attempted to strike a balance between hard work and fun. Still, those early days came with many challenges. Though the students remained upbeat, I could tell we had major mental hurdles to overcome.

Before my arrival, Spelman didn't offer any mobile robotics courses. So I not only had to instruct the students on how to program the robots to compete in the soccer matches, but I also needed to teach the team the fundamentals of AIBO coding. I knew that if I could get the students comfortable enough to teach the robots how to walk, sit, and push we might have a fighting chance. But I felt we were at an impasse. Without the benefit of any previous robotics courses, my team members were at a psychological deficit.

"Dear Lord," I said one morning before a busy day, "please help our team to qualify for RoboCup. Just like everything else, I can't do anything without You. But with You, I can do anything." As with my marriage and my dissertation, I knew the only way I was going to crack the code was by the grace of God. "I need You, Lord."

Then two things happened that served to motivate our spirits and get us on track. First, Dave Touretzky, a research professor in computer science at Carnegie Mellon University in Pittsburgh, called me because he had heard from a female colleague that Spelman College had a good computer science department. When he called to find out if there might be some possibility of collaborating on research, our chair referred him to me. I picked up the phone, heard his name, and nearly fell out of my chair. I knew that Dave Touretzky was a leading scholar in the field of cognitive robotics. And, as it turns out, he invented Tekkotsu—the robotics-programming platform that I had used in Iowa and that we were trying to use at Spelman. For me, being on the phone with the guy was like talking to a movie star.

After some brief chitchat about our respective areas of research, I said: "Hey, by the way, we're trying to take a team to the International RoboCup!" But that fell kind of flat. Dave wasn't particularly interested in getting robots to play soccer. However, as I told him about the uniqueness of our team, and the fact that my team members were trying to learn Tekkotsu without the benefit of a previous robotics course, he seemed to perk up.

Some brief background: The Sony AIBO comes with a software interface called the Open-R SDK Development Kit. It gives you everything you need to move different motors and joints and to program the sensors, but it's on a very low level. Tekkotsu, which is Japanese for "iron bones," is built on top of the Open-R SDK application and is able to accept more high-level commands. With his work in cognitive robotics, Dave specializes in high-level programming that enables users to program various robotic functions such as locomotion (movement from one place to another) and localization (the ability to sense where they are in relation to the rest of their known environment). Having the SpelBots learn directly from Dave would be akin to a piano student getting one-on-one instruction from Beethoven. So I rephrased my question.

"Would you be interested in coming to Spelman to give a workshop on Tekkotsu?" I asked. He didn't even hesitate: "Absolutely."

So Dave and his graduate assistant, Ethan Tira-Thompson, came down to Atlanta on three separate occasions to conduct a series of workshops. We were all impressed with his amazing grasp of robotics and the ease with which he was able to convey his knowledge to all of us. And I was thankful that this brilliant scientist would graciously give of his time and effort to help prepare and inspire my students.

The second thing that got us on track was the fallout related to a controversial speech delivered in January 2005 by Harvard University president Lawrence Summers. While speaking at an economics conference, Summers, who had already sparked widespread unrest at Harvard with his iconoclastic style of leadership, suggested that the under representation of female scientists at the top colleges and universities might stem from "innate" differences between men and women. The overwhelming insinuation of his words: women are not genetically wired as well as men to do science and mathematics on a high level.

Summers set off a firestorm of debate in academia and throughout the nation, with some people insisting that there was academic validity to his point and others calling it shortsighted at best and sexist at worst. He left Harvard the following year amid lingering criticism, after only five years on the job.

What Summers's words did for me was to remind me that there are people out there who would still put others in a box because of their race, gender, class, or physical condition. Being at Spelman and seeing the immense intelligence and potential of my students made the fallacy of "the box" even more clear to me. And it stirred within me, and many of my students, a stronger resolve to not just prove the naysayers wrong, but to prove God right.

The Bible says that God shows no partiality (Acts 10:34); He loves us all the same and is, I believe, an equal-opportunity God. The Bible also says, in the words of the apostle Paul: "There is neither Jew nor Greek, there is neither slave nor free man, there is neither male nor female; for you are all one in Christ Jesus" (Galatians 3:28). Though we may put limits on each other due to things like race and gender, God does not observe such restricting divisions among His people.

In some ways, Summers's words reminded me of the controversy surrounding *The Bell Curve* a decade earlier. In that infamous book, two social scientists argued that race could be a determining factor in one's level of intelligence, and that people of African descent might be academically inferior due to genetics. As a biracial person who saw firsthand how race was sometimes used to prejudge or keep certain people out, this opinion troubled me deeply. I knew that people were more than the color of their skin or the location of their neighborhood. And it was the same with gender.

Summers helped me remember why I had come to Spelman in

the first place and motivated me to persevere through the slog of inexperience, discipline, and uncertainty to lead my students to a higher plane of ability and purpose.

Thanks in part to Dave Touretzky and Lawrence Summers, the SpelBots triumphed over early adversity and moved on to even greater challenges.

CHAPTER 14

Success Is Never Final

Our progress was steady and true. Once the team picked up the essentials of Tekkotsu, it was a new day. Our afternoon meetings went from hours of watching the clock slowly tick by to suddenly wondering where on earth the time went. And the women regained that extra spring in their steps that a college student needs as she's preparing to change the world. It was encouraging to witness the emergence from our collective fear of the unknown.

Regarding the drudgery of the learning curve, MIT management scholar Edgar Schein said something like this: "We often resist learning new things because, as we do, we become temporarily incompetent."

I think he's right. Learning something new requires us to willingly enter into a state of helplessness, until we're able to absorb enough information to regain a sense of control. It's never fun at first, but it's the only way to grow.

For a while, the SpelBots had to immerse themselves in an unfamiliar system, stripping away any sense of power, in order to eventually take command of some new skills. Thankfully, they persevered and were soon stronger for it.

The Starting Lineup

Over the spring semester and the beginning of the summer, I saw the team develop a fresh sense of confidence that elevated their abilities to a new level. In the process, I also learned more about this incredible team of young women.

In the New Testament, the apostle Paul talks about the diversity of the church body and the unique and necessary gifts that each member brings to the mix. I've witnessed this wonderful phenomenon many times in the churches I've attended, where young and old, hip and square, black and white all manage to get along and support each other in profound and unexpected ways, despite their differences. That Scripture passage says: "And the eye cannot say to the hand, 'I have no need of you'; or again the head to the feet, 'I have no need of you.' And if one member suffers, all the members suffer with it; if one member is honored, all the members rejoice with it" (1 Corinthians 12:21, 26). This became true for the Spel-Bots, too, as we worked together as one, each member contributing her own special part to the whole.

Our seniors, Aryen Moore-Alston and Brandy Kinlaw, both gave important leadership to the team in their own ways. As our captain, and probably the most outgoing student on the team, Aryen was our top spokesperson. Her greatest strength for our team was her organizational and communication skills. Though originally from Memphis, Aryen spent part of her childhood in Italy, and a year in Japan through Spelman's Study Abroad program, so she was a proficient speaker of both Italian and Japanese—language skills I knew would come in handy if we qualified to go to Japan. Having recently lost my mom, I empathized with Aryen when I learned she had lost her dad as a child. In addition to the SpelBots, she was an ardent Spelman dance student. In fact, her true passion may have resided more with dance than science. Still, she was an extremely capable student of computer science, and her internship experience at the NASA Jet Propulsion Lab gave her a solid understanding of the amount of discipline and hard work that would be required to master the AIBO.

Brandy excelled as our lead programmer, especially after our workshops with Dave Touretzky. Early on, she came to the computer lab on weekends determined to master Tekkotsu and figure out how to do the high-level programming we needed. Brandy was from Goldsboro, North Carolina, and like all the SpelBots was an excellent student with a friendly personality. On a basketball team, there's always a go-to player, that clutch performer who always steps up when the game is on the line; out of all the SpelBots, Brandy was our "go-to" robot programmer. When the chips were down, you could count on Brandy racking her brain to figure out how to get the robot to do what we needed it to do.

Shinese Noble was a hard-working student from Long Island who had New York toughness but Atlanta friendliness. She was excellent at fixing things with her hands. Whenever we faced mechanical problems, Shinese was the one who took charge. She was the only SpelBot member who volunteered to join the team after hearing about it through word of mouth from someone other than me.

I was surprised that Ebony Smith wasn't already doing research with a professor before I met her in my Data Structures and Algorithms class. Also from Memphis, she was a natural-born leader and our second best programmer after Brandy. Ebony, who became one of my student assistants, worked with me on the bioinformatics research that I continued from Iowa.

Both Ebony O'Neal and Karina Liles were in the Model Institutions for Excellence (MIE) program at Spelman and were assigned to work with me in robotics. The pair was best friends and virtually inseparable. It didn't take either of them long to pick up on the programming concepts once we got going.

Ebony, who was from nearby Barnesville, Georgia, was very active in the Spelman spiritual community. When I asked for a volunteer to lead our team in prayer, she would be the one to volunteer. She wasn't shy, but she was definitely the SpelBot's most low-key member.

Karina hailed from Bennettsville, South Carolina. If Ebony was the quiet one, then Karina was on the other end of the spectrum, which perhaps explains why the two were so close. Karina, like all of the SpelBots, was extremely bright, but she also possessed a great sense of humor. She often used laughter to keep the team's spirits lifted during stressful moments. And there were plenty of stressful moments.

While there were certainly tension and conflict, as you might expect in any family-like group where people spend countless hours together, overall the team members got along exceptionally well. It helped that we had a common goal, and that each member loved computers and technology. Still, I needed to find ways to maintain and build upon the momentum we had recently attained.

The Theme Is Courage

To keep the team motivated, I regularly preached what I felt should be the ultimate aim of any collegiate robotics team—competing in the International RoboCup. To some, it probably seemed naïve or overly ambitious to think we could rise to the international level in just our first year of competition. But I believe it's important to set impossible goals and work like crazy to meet them. I know; when you aim that high, the chances of missing the mark are multiplied. But where you end up after the dust settles will undoubtedly be further along than where you would've been had you acted more cautiously.

The 2005 RoboCup was set to take place in Osaka, Japan, and I knew it would require a substantial amount of cash to get all six students there. So, from the beginning, I set the challenge before the team: "If we qualify for the finals, we'll need to raise support to go because traveling to Japan is going to be extremely expensive." Who cares that we had yet to compete in a single match? I wanted the SpelBots to begin envisioning themselves as a team whose path to Japan was inevitable.

"You're right," said Aryen, who had been to Japan. "It could take as much as $1,200 just to buy a plane ticket."

"How are we going to get that much money?" Brandy asked.

"I think you guys should work up a special presentation for President Tatum," I said. "We need to show her what we're trying to do. Once she catches the vision, maybe the college will help fund our travel, assuming we qualify."

The team agreed and began to develop a presentation. With Aryen leading the way, over the next few days the team worked to craft a PowerPoint show and a demonstration of the AIBO's motion capabilities using a dance downloaded from the Internet.

Spelman's president, Dr. Beverly Daniel Tatum, came to the college in 2002. Before that, she had been a longtime professor of psychology at Mount Holyoke College in Massachusetts where she was also a dean and, before her departure, the acting president. Dr. Tatum is widely known for her groundbreaking books on race relations, including *"Why Are All the Black Kids Sitting Together in the Cafeteria?" And Other Conversations About Race*, which explores issues of racial identity among high school and college students.

Throughout the academic year, President Tatum held open office hours, where she invited anyone from the campus community to come in and talk. It was an excellent opportunity to have an audience with the busiest woman on campus.

So, we gathered our gear and visited President Tatum during the open hours. The students introduced themselves and then talked about robotics and artificial intelligence, their interest in science, and the RoboCup competitions in which we planned to participate—including how much it was going to cost for us to travel to Japan, should we make the cut. We could see genuine interest rising in Dr. Tatum's eyes as we presented a live demonstration of the robot dancing, which offered a visible measure of the AIBO's capabilities. The students did an excellent job.

President Tatum was so impressed that she promised to find funding for the travel of all six SpelBot students and two faculty members, if we qualified for the International RoboCup. What's more, she agreed to buy us four additional robots (at $2,000 each) to allow the team to run intrateam scrimmages.

President Tatum made good on her promise and was able to secure $50,000 of funding from the Coca-Cola Foundation. In addition, Ted Aronson, a generous Spelman College advisory board member, cheerfully gave $25,000 for our team to travel to Japan with instructions to "make sure we ate some sushi." God blessed our team abundantly through wonderful people like Dr. Tatum and Mr. Aronson, and was answering our prayers of faith. (The extra funds would allow Spelman to hire a documentary film crew led by a seasoned professional, Bryan Simmons, to help document our journey.)

In order to qualify for the 2005 International RoboCup tournament, we had to send in our technical application in February and await our selection into the international competition. In our technical application, we stated our intent to participate in both the U.S. Open and in the international competition, along with how we were going to design and implement the various robotic functions required for the AIBOs to play autonomous soccer. The technical questions we had to answer included how we were going to give our robots computer vision, the ability to kick and move from place to place, how we were going to implement our artificial intelligence for decision making, and how we were going to perform localization (i.e., give our robots the ability to determine where they were at on the robot soccer playing field). Our first competition would be at the U.S. RoboCup, which would take place in May, just down the road from Spelman at the Georgia Institute of Technology (a.k.a. Georgia Tech).

With a renewed determination, and a fresh out-of-the-box set of new AIBOs, we went to work. The SpelBots members sought to spend on average ten hours each week programming and training the robots in preparation for the U.S. RoboCup, but some of them spent much longer that that. The SpelBots were still only undergrad students, but they worked as if they were already in grad school. However, unlike graduate students, who could devote most of their time to research, our students had to carve out time in between their classes, homework, and other extracurricular activities.

Later on, in preparation for the International RoboCup, they would work at least forty hours a week.

The students would come to the computer lab throughout the day and night to work on their various assignments. Some would arrive early in the morning; others would put in time late at night. In fact, though this is humbling to confess, collectively the students probably knew more about programming the robots than I did. But, as I often told folks, the SpelBots is a student-centered endeavor; I was just the adviser and coach. Like Tony Dungy in the NFL, I sought to bring out the best from my "players" so that they would be prepared for the "game." Since the Tekkotsu software they were using was open source and we knew its creator, the students could always e-mail or call Professor Touretzky or his assistant, Ethan Tira-Thompson, with questions whenever they were stumped. Dave and Ethan were careful to remind the students that they didn't want to interfere with the competition, since Carnegie Mellon had their own RoboCup team (even though they were not a part of it). While the students were calling on the Tekkotsu "creators," I was constantly calling upon my Creator to give us the wisdom and grace to make it through this pressure-packed time.

As I watched the students rise to the challenge of preparing to compete with the best AIBO programmers in the nation, I beamed with pride. I saw their hard work and dedication, and I knew that anything less than qualifying for the Osaka tournament would be a crushing blow to the team. So, I decided to share with them some timeless wisdom that was imparted to me when I was an undergraduate. At the start of one of our late-afternoon meetings, I scribbled these lines on the white dry-erase board:

Success is never final. Failure is seldom fatal.
But it's courage that counts.

"Ladies, as we dive deeper into this process, it's going to get increasingly intense," I told the team. "That's why I want each of you to remember these words from Winston Churchill."

I asked the students to read the words aloud with me: "Success is never final. Failure is seldom fatal. But it's courage that counts."

I continued, "These are words that helped me navigate some crazy times in college. If you haven't figured it out yet, I was a bit of a perfectionist in school. I took losses and setbacks particularly hard. So when a Bible teacher shared this quote with my campus ministry group, it really stuck with me. In fact, I made it my personal motto. And I think it might be good to make Churchill's quote the SpelBots' theme for our march to the RoboCup.

"Whatever happens, I want each of you to remember that you should never define yourself by winning or losing, but rather by how you pursued your goal. Did you give it your best effort? Did you play the game with integrity? Did you treat your teammates and opponents with kindness and respect? When it's all said and done, your character is what matters more than anything else."

I could tell the students were starting to get that glazed-over look that young people get when a parent or teacher rattles on too long, so I ended my speech there. However, as a reminder, I left Churchill's words on the computer-lab board for the remainder of the semester.

Showdown at Georgia Tech

May is an intense month for college students, especially seniors. Between final exams, graduation, securing summer or permanent employment, and preparing to vacate the campus, these are taxing times. For the SpelBot members, however, an already busy season became even busier with the addition of the RoboCup U.S. Open.

With final exams so close, the SpelBots had to prep themselves for their first real competition with outside opponents. Thankfully, the 2005 tournament was just a few miles away at Georgia Tech.

Thirty teams composed of more than 200 collegiate researchers gathered for the event. The tournament features five different robotics events, four of which are soccer-based. The fifth is a search-

and-rescue competition in which teams remotely direct robots to find victims in a simulated disaster scene. The soccer events use both humanoid robots and the four-legged canine variety, which tend to be the most popular.

The four-legged, four-on-four version of the game operates a lot like a real-life soccer match. There's the nineteen-foot field with goal boxes, colored landmarks, and a center circle. Plus, referees dish out penalties against the AIBOs, and their owners, for pushing and obstruction. One AIBO on each team is programmed to be the goalie.

During the three-day event, we were scheduled to face Georgia Tech, the University of Texas–Austin, and Columbia University of New York. It was fascinating to watch the other schools go about their business of programming their own AIBOs. The SpelBots were probably a tad bit intimidated at first. After all, this was their first time out. The ladies immediately detected the confidence and swagger of the veteran teams that filled the arena. Everyone knew that we had our work cut out for us.

The AIBOs are not remote-controlled but run off a user-defined program installed on a memory stick inserted into their tummies. The information on the memory stick instructs the robots on how to react to the events around them. Each AIBO has a video camera in its nose that the computer program on the memory stick processes using segmentation algorithms based on mathematics. This "computer vision" is used to detect the presence and location of the apple-sized ball as well as the goals, landmarks, and other robots on the field.

The AIBOs have to use their artificial intelligence to decide how and when to pass the ball to each other. They come equipped with wireless cards that can be used for interrobot communication, as well as to communicate with the referee for start and penalty information. As humans, we take for granted that we have the ability to see or walk or make decisions. Giving robots the ability to see, walk, and think are ongoing research areas. Every time I think about the complexities of these abilities that we humans are given,

I am in awe of our great Creator.

The RoboCup actually involves more than just the games. Teams qualify for the various events by passing a series of technical tests. We also were required to present a demonstration of our technical skills at the conclusion of the competition. Taken together, it was an exhausting process.

During these times, I prayed often. I tried not to force my beliefs on the SpelBots members, but they all knew I was a committed Christian. Though I never attempted to "convert" any of the team members, I was able to share my faith with them in real-life settings. It has always been important to me to be a role model, to show others how faith can be lived out in normal, everyday life.

At various times during our meetings or before some milestone event, such as our presentation to President Tatum, I asked the team to join me in prayers for God's favor and direction. On many of those occasions, Ebony S. and Ebony O. volunteered to lead us in prayer. I made sure that all the students were comfortable with us praying because I wanted to always remain respectful of others' beliefs, whether they were religious or nonreligious. I knew that two Christian women had started Spelman and that the school's motto on its official logo was "Our Whole School for Christ."

However, I also knew that Spelman recognizes that the world offers a diversity of beliefs and religions and wants all students to feel welcome. With that in mind, I felt comfortable living out my faith at Spelman. For me, praying with the SpelBots was as natural as teaching them how to program robots. If we were going to be a unified, cohesive unit, God needed to be a part of it. So, before each of our matches, we formed a circle, joined hands, and spoke to God.

Our first match against Georgia Tech was nerve-racking. It was our first real competition, so naturally the team was jittery. Still, they came ready to play. Though we lost 0 to 1, our goalie did manage to block a shot—partly because it had a program crash. It was a funny, ironic moment for us. We were happy that we were able to have such a close match against such a prestigious engineering school as Georgia Tech.

Our big objective that first time out was to simply get the dogs to function. As Ebony O. later said, "We wanted to see what would transpire with research done in the lab with what would take place on the actual playing field." The AIBOs didn't always perform in the way the women had tried to program them. At times, they responded sluggishly or went in the wrong direction, almost like a stubborn pet. Though the AIBOs were just machines, after working with them for so long, the students had developed true affection for the little creatures. "It's almost like an adult watching their child play a game," Aryen later told *Ebony* magazine about the RoboCup experience.[4]

During that first match, Tucker Balch, the Georgia Tech robotics professor who organized the event, announced that the SpelBots was the first all-women team to compete in RoboCup. President Tatum, who was in attendance with other faculty and staff, beamed with pride. She was especially supportive of me personally as the pressure intensified. She once told me, "Don't worry, Andrew. It's so unusual for our college to be competing in these robotic events. It reminds me of that first time that the Jamaican bobsled team competed in the Olympics." We both laughed as I realized that she said exactly what I needed to hear at that moment.

We had a few hours to work out the kinks before our second event. So, we went to work trying to enhance the robots' vision. The AIBOs' vision was sensitive to various levels of lighting and had to be calibrated according to the lighting environment we were in. This was critical for the robots to be able to see objects on the field correctly, like the orange soccer ball. We saw some minor improvements in our second match, but we still fell to Texas, 0 to 5. Dr. Peter Stone, a Carnegie Mellon–trained professor who was a recognized leader in machine learning, led their team. He gave us encouragement by letting us know that the first time they competed in RoboCup, they couldn't score a single goal.

The following day, in our final match against Columbia University, we struggled again but kept our composure and continued plugging away. During the first half of the match, our robots caught sight of the ball more consistently and pursued it at a slow, choppy pace. All of a sudden Brandy exclaimed, "Oh he sees it!" Aryen yelled, "Go, go, go! Get it! Get it! Get it!" Miraculously, Columbia's goalie had done a handstand and inadvertently became stuck on its head. Another one of their defenders tried to come back to block our SpelBot, but the referee removed it because it was illegally defending the goal by occupying the space only the goalie could occupy. Our SpelBot had a clear path to the goal—and we scored! We had actually scored, in the first half, before Columbia did. Our SpelBot canines executed a choppy but effective sequence of kicks that resulted in a successful goal. We cheered and jumped up and down like we'd won the world championships. Though we lost 1 to 2, we left Georgia Tech with our heads mostly up.

That late-game score gave us the extra morale boost we needed going forward. We thought it would take until the International RoboCup in Japan before we would be able to score a goal, but we did it at the U.S. Open. We had exceeded our goals and expectations.

There were several good things to take away from the U.S. RoboCup experience. For starters, the SpelBots became the first all-women team and the first group representing an HBCU to compete in a RoboCup. But more practically, our participation in the contest gave us a chance to see how the "big boys" played the game. Their focus, determination, and ability to think on their feet were excellent attributes to emulate.

The fact that Georgia Tech and Texas each had Ph.D. students on their teams and that Texas had worked on its programming code for the last three years was not lost on any of us. We had managed to hang in there with teams that should've been light-years ahead of us, and that was a reaffirming message to carry us to our next challenge.

Ebony S. later said: "Georgia Tech was like a trial run for us, the first competition we took seriously. Seeing what our dogs did, we used that as motivation for going to Japan."

In Osaka, we would try to avoid the bad stuff and improve on the good.

CHAPTER 15

From Georgia to Japan

Prior to competing at the U.S. Open, we learned that Spelman had made the short list for the International RoboCup in Osaka. The RoboCup Technical Committee sent an e-mail to all the teams that had qualified for the Four-Legged Competition. My heart started to thump noticeably in my chest as my eyes walked down the list of teams that had made the cut. Spelman was in!

I sent an e-mail to the team and called them on the phone to let them know we had an urgent meeting. As we met, I began to read the e-mail with a very somber face. There were twelve teams that had prequalified by their performance at RoboCup the year before. Then there was the list of teams that had qualified by a review of their technical application and videos of their AIBOs playing soccer. The e-mail read, ". . . Les 3 Mousquetaires, MiPal, SpelBots . . ." The students let out a collective scream and we all high-fived each other. I asked the team if I could say a prayer of thanks to acknowledge God's grace, and we all bowed our heads.

We had earned a spot in the tournament by submitting a technical application, which included video footage that documented our research and technical approach.

Out of thirty-three robotics teams from around the world that had applied to compete in the competition, only twenty-four teams made the cut for the four-legged soccer matches. The teams came from the U.S., Europe, South America, Asia, and Australia. So we were in rarefied territory—the first all-women's school and the first African American institution to achieve this honor. Our six trail-blazing students continued to make computer-engineering history. Without a doubt, I knew people were going to notice an all-female, African American robotics team in Japan. Now, everything we had studied and sweated for was right before us.

I thought back to all my years of striving and struggle, of know-ing that God had a special call on my life, but not knowing quite how to get there. I thought about all the near misses—with rela-tionships, pride, rebellion, perfectionism, ignorance—things that could've derailed this dream. Instead, God protected, guided, and provided. Through no merit of my own, He continually led me to the next level of ministry and service—until, finally, I found myself in the privileged position of leading a diverse crew of young, gifted African American women to a place where no other group of black women had been before. What an honor. And what a ride!

Not only did President Tatum make good on her promise to fund our trip to Osaka, securing the Coca-Cola Foundation spon-sorship and receiving support from board member Ted Aronson, but she decided to tag along herself. I could tell she was as proud and excited as I was to see the SpelBots take this world stage in col-legiate robotics.

Also joining us on our ten-day trip overseas were President Tatum's husband, Dr. Travis Tatum, and her son, David Tatum; Ebony S.'s mother, Brenda Smith; Shinese's mother, Rene Moore; and my wonderful wife (once again, we scuttled the kids to Kansas City to stay with my brother George and his wife, Trudy). We also had other members of the Spelman College family as well as our documentary crew. This would be a trip to remember.

Tokyo Touchdown

The International RoboCup was scheduled for July 13 to 19. Our twelve-hour flight from Atlanta touched down in Tokyo on July 11. We decided to spend a couple days relaxing—and shopping—in Tokyo before continuing our trek to Osaka. I had been to Tokyo earlier that year for the National Academy of Engineering's Frontiers of Engineering conference, so Japan was not completely new to me. But except for Aryen and me, it was everyone else's first time in the island nation.

Upon arriving in the city, one is immediately struck by the sheer multitude of people and their nonstop movement—the rush of hurried bodies, pushing and shoving to get to and fro. It was sometimes a challenge keeping our group of students and family intact, though we did tend to stick out like a sore thumb.

For the uninitiated, Japan is thoroughly foreign to the senses— the sights, sounds, smells, and prices (very expensive!). Though we were an ethnic spectacle among the plethora of Japanese faces, the people were tremendously warm and friendly to us. Many times on the train or at a restaurant, our students would be asked to pose for photos with mesmerized strangers. When we told them we were competing in the RoboCup, they were even more enthralled.

Though the people were generally very courteous, at one point we were trying to board a train when a Japanese man told Shinese to go to the end of the line because he thought she was cutting in front of him. He only spoke Japanese, but we understood his thumb signal and the big frown on his face. Awkwardly enough, I wound up sitting by the unhappy man on the train, and I could feel the tension in the air around us. Our group laughed and tried to break the tension, but the man wasn't amused. Shinese took a picture of me sitting by the man: I'm smiling and he's frowning as he leans away from me.

But there were many other warmer moments. At a mall, a Japanese women gave us a bag of grapes as a gift when she found out we were from America. Later, an elderly Japanese man saw our

Spelman students and repeated, in his broken English, "I like Beyoncé! I like Beyoncé!"

As we explored the city, Anitra and I remembered our old friend Nobuhiro Yoshizawa, the GE engineer from Japan who had helped me learn bits and pieces of his language and culture. A few of the phrases he taught me—such as *Toire wa, doko desu ka?*—actually came in handy during our trip. (For the curious, that means "Where is the toilet?".)

Thankfully, though, the group was not reliant on my Japanese; we had Aryen at our disposal with her outstanding language skills. She was able to assist the group by asking directions, translating signs, and ordering from menus on our behalf whenever they were in Japanese only and had no pictures. Truly, if anyone earned her keep on this trip, it was Aryen, who had to be "on" every waking second in order to help the rest of us survive.

And then there was the food.

Our hotels had both an American and a Japanese/Asian buffet. None of us were accustomed to eating fish and rice for breakfast. However, since my mom occasionally made Korean food for my siblings and me back in the day, we ate lots of rice growing up, so it wasn't too much of an adjustment for me.

One of the students (I won't mention her name) had a challenging time adjusting to the Japanese cuisine and longed for a familiar American meal. She had brought plenty of snacks from home to live on, just in case. And we were glad to find her a McDonald's in Osaka that was not far from the hotel. But even there they served a teriyaki burger that caused several students to long for a good, old-fashioned American Big Mac.

The first night we arrived in Tokyo, we gathered for a special dinner at a quaint, sparsely lit restaurant. We were all exhausted from the fourteen-hour Delta flight from Atlanta to Tokyo. We were served traditional Japanese food, such as rice, miso soup, and grilled fish. And though some had problems enjoying the food, it was actually quite good. During the meal, I asked the people around the table to share a few words about their experiences so far, and what it meant for them to be there.

Each of the SpelBots members spoke about the trip's significance to them. They were excited to be testing their skills against the best collegiate programmers in the world. They cherished the opportunity to visit a storied and exotic locale like Japan. And each of them expressed pride at the prospect of becoming role models for other African American girls who might be interested in science, computers, and technology.

Brenda Smith cried as she revealed how proud she was of her daughter—and all the team members. "All of you have such a great future ahead of you," she said. "Thanks for letting me be a part of it with Ebony."

Finally, I told the team members that, no matter what happened the next day at the tournament, they were already winners. "Newspapers, CNN, *Ebony* magazine, and scientific journals are all telling your story because they realize how exceptional you are," I said. "But this is only the beginning."

I reminded them of our team motto and they joined me in reciting it. And save for a few faltering voices at the beginning, they all knew it: "Success is never final. Failure is seldom fatal. But it's courage that counts."

I told the team, "Keep that in mind in these coming days. You all have shown a lot of courage. And again, courage is not the absence of fear but in the midst of some fear not letting it paralyze you but having faith that you'll make it through."

Our Osaka Odyssey

We awoke extra early the next morning, even though all of us were still feeling the effects of the thirteen-hour time difference between Tokyo and Atlanta. The food, jet lag, and culture shock had all taken their toll, but each of us knew how important the coming days were. Focusing on the momentous events ahead of us got our adrenaline flowing soon enough.

The trip south to Osaka was an adventure as we waited for and boarded the Shinkansen, the Japanese bullet train that travels up to 130 miles per hour. While we were waiting, Ebony O. and Karina had Anitra and me act out a skit they wrote. In the skit, we had to celebrate by dancing. Little did we know, they were secretly filming our dance moves so they could show it to others later.

We needed to take three additional trains to make it to the site of the RoboCup—and all while lugging around our robots, computers, and peripheral equipment. The trains felt like human sardine cans, as we became crushed in the unrelenting swarm of busy commuters. Our hotel in Osaka was connected to the city's busiest train station, where more than a million people passed through each day.

Despite the obstacles, we made it to the party on time. At the Intex Osaka, an international exhibition center, the floor was abuzz with the energy and excitement of the three hundred teams from thirty-one countries that were competing in the various soccer and search-and-rescue contests. Concurrently, a huge Japanese robot trade show was also taking place. In all, the estimates of people visiting the center that week would reach in the hundreds of thousands.

From a quick survey of the environment, I could tell this challenge would be even greater than the one we had faced at Georgia Tech. These international programmers represented the very best in graduate-level robotics. Many of these people would be the ones to help the RoboCup Federation meet their stated goal for the organization. According to its mission information, "By 2050, a team of fully autonomous humanoid robot soccer players shall win a soccer game, complying with the official [international soccer] rules, against the winner of the most recent World Cup of Human Soccer."

In other words, in forty-five years the RoboCup visionaries believed our technology would be advanced enough to field a team of lifelike robots that could successfully defeat the best human teams in the world. That probably seems like an outrageous and unlikely aim, but only for those who don't spend most of their time engaged in robotics research and engineering. Indeed, the current research is so promising that scientists might actually beat that 2050 goal by a few years.

On the surface, the RoboCup perhaps looks like a roomful of nerdy computer geniuses wasting time with fun and games, but at its core the competition is really about the practice and execution of serious research with far-reaching implications for fields such as medicine and physiotherapy. For instance, the technology may eventually allow engineers to create robots that can autonomously assist elderly or physically disabled humans with simple and complex tasks. Or, robots might help physically incapacitated victims of accidents to rehab their injuries without the need for human assistants.

These are real and achievable goals toward which progress is being made every day, and the students and researchers that populate the RoboCup events are the innovative minds that will someday take robotics to that next level of artificial intelligence. Which is one reason why it was so important for me to see women and students of color playing an active part in the RoboCup proceedings.

Finding our spot on the floor, we unpacked our equipment, set up our station, and unleashed the AIBOs for what would be the most significant challenge of the SpelBots' brief existence. Our first opponent would be the NuBots from Australia. Their team was a serious contender for the championship.

As team captain, Aryen conferred with the referees and her counterpart from the NuBots to go over the rules. Brandy mobilized the team in readying the AIBOs. Performing the color calibration for the AIBOs' video camera sensors was of the utmost importance. Also, the rest of the team had to ensure the batteries were charged and that the correct cards were properly inserted into each mechanical pup.

This time out, the team was still nervous but no longer intimidated. Our experience in the U.S. RoboCup had given us the confidence needed to approach the competition knowing that we belonged there, too.

By the time we formed a circle to pray, I could tell the team was ready. We thanked God for allowing us and the other teams to arrive in Osaka safely. We prayed for patience and a spirit of teamwork. And we asked God to settle our nerves as our SpelBot pups took to the soccer field.

Suddenly, I felt a strong sense of peace and calm about the day's events. Even though a part of me wanted to see our autonomous dogs block opposing shots, pass the ball effortlessly, and take over the game at will, I was content to know that we had the skill and fortitude to compete on this stage. I knew that our success would not depend on whether we won or lost, but on the courage and integrity with which we approached the contest.

A Bigger Victory

We fought hard, and our quartet of AIBOs mounted a credible challenge to the opposing four-legged machines. However, even in the early minutes of the match, everyone could see that our robots were just a step slower than what would be needed to battle on this level. During time-outs, Brandy and Ebony S. led their teammates in grabbing the robots and fixing them up, like a NASCAR pit crew. The team worked feverishly to re-program our dogs for enhanced speed and stronger localization. And everyone could see the progressive improvement throughout the match.

But in the end, it wasn't enough. We eventually lost the match, 10 to 0. Though the SpelBots put up a valiant effort, we were clearly overmatched by a more seasoned team of graduate-level programmers.

In fact, the NuBots had taken third place in the International RoboCup each of the last three years. "These guys are ranked No. 3 in the world, and could very well be the eventual champions," I told the team members, who were visibly disappointed.

"I'm just happy to be here," said Ebony S., smiling so she wouldn't cry. "But I'd be even happier if we could've scored just *one* goal."

In our remaining two matches against the BabyTigers from

Japan and DutchAIBO, a team from the Netherlands, our margins of loss were less. Though we still failed to score a victory, we saw a gradual improvement, and I was proud of my students.

"Remember what we've been saying for the past eight months?" I told the team. "Success is not final and failure is not fatal. You women have made history here this week And this is only the beginning." I could only imagine the African American women back in the U.S. who would be giving our team a standing ovation had they been able to view our match and the obstacles that we had overcome.

We all hugged and shared a laugh, and I reiterated how proud I was of everyone. Slowly our sense of purpose and the deeper joy of our accomplishment broke through the temporary dejection, and reminded each of us that our participation in the RoboCup wasn't about scoring points but building a foundation for future Spelman students, and African American women in general, to play more active roles in the fields of science, math, and engineering. I told the SpelBots, "You are now the researchers and programmers that my daughters and other young girls will read about, and say, 'I want to do that, too.' And that's a far bigger victory than any amount of goals we could've scored on the soccer field."

President Tatum reminded us of how remarkable it was that we were there. "You women only formed the team eight or nine months ago, and now here you are!" She added, "Your pathbreaking accomplishments will shine a light to young women for years to come."

Back home in the United States, as word spread about the achievements of the SpelBots, the team received more media coverage and a slew of invitations to share their story and encourage future generations of female scientists.

The SpelBots' influence spread much faster and wider than I could've ever imagined. I was able to write a National Science Foundation (NSF) proposal and receive hundreds of thousands of dollars of funding to partner with Dave Touretzky and Carnegie

Mellon to start our C.A.R.E. project (Computer and Robotics Education for African Americans) through NSF's Broadening Participation in Computing program. Later, the C.A.R.E. project resulted in another grant that I shared with faculty members from other HBCUs and major research institutions to begin the ARTSI Alliance[5] (Advancing Robotics Technology for Societal Impact). This endeavor netted millions of dollars in NSF funding, along with generous underwriting from Google, Seagate, Intel, and Apple.

Though thrilled at its rapid success, I was not completely surprised by the SpelBots' impact. Once again, I recalled that special verse from 2 Chronicles that had become a rallying cry for my life: "For the eyes of the Lord move to and fro throughout the earth that He may strongly support those whose heart is completely His."

CHAPTER 16

The SpelBots 2.0

M any people still wonder why I would come to Spelman from a Big Ten major research institution. "You aren't following the traditional academic career path," some have told me. Or, "Why are you teaching at an HBCU, let alone an HBCU for women?"

When it comes down to it, it was because of my love for God and my passion for learning. I decided that one reason God made me was to uplift and enable African American young people academically, vocationally, spiritually, and economically.

Today it thrills me to know that my original SpelBots, each in her own way, are on track to continue making history. Aryen, for instance, worked at a technology consulting company and is now pursuing her passion for acting and dance choreography. She recently hosted a local TV show. Brandy went on to get her master's degree in computer science and now in Memphis works as a software engineer. Shinese's love for computer science was reaffirmed by her SpelBots experience; she finished her master's degree in Internet Technology with an emphasis in e-commerce and currently works in New York. Ebony S., who dreams of one day curing diseases, went on to get her master's degree in bioinformatics and recently started pursuing medicine in an M.D./Ph.D. program. And Ebony O. and Karina finished their degrees in computer science and are pursuing their professional careers.

As for my family, although the SpelBots dominated our world throughout my first year at Spelman College, there were other notable experiences as well. We found a wonderful family of Christians at Mount Calvary Missionary Baptist Church, where Anitra and I serve as Sunday school teachers for the young adults. Also, Anitra is helping our children transition from being homeschooled to attending both public and private schools. John, Adrianna, and Rosa all stay busy in a variety of extracurricular activities like music, gymnastics, and golf. And Anitra is continuing to nurture our kids and guide them in their education while she works as a specialist at a local Apple Retail Store.

Still T.E.A.C.H.ing

Today my outreach to college students continues, as I work with various campus ministry groups to encourage students and point them to the ultimate source of success in life. God even reconnected me with Tony Gatewood, the eager young man whom I mentored when he was a student at the University of Iowa. Tony is now a campus minister for InterVarsity Christian Fellowship and leads groups at Morehouse and Spelman.

I also quietly continue to share my faith through relationship evangelism. While I would never impose my faith upon my students or beat them over the head with my beliefs, I do feel it's my privilege and responsibility to model what a Christian is like for those around me who do not believe. I always pray that my marriage and parenting are positive examples for my students to witness. I pray for all my students and colleagues, discuss questions about spiritual issues, and invite them to visit my church. One of my students even made the decision to become a Christian, which was a powerful reminder of God's call on my life to T.E.A.C.H.[6]

The SpelBots have certainly endured some growing pains. It's only natural that interest in an extracurricular activity requiring such a huge commitment will have its clashes—with fun things college students get involved in, in learning how to deal with team chemistry issues, with leadership challenges, or within other problems that arise when being a coach and a mentor. We've had our struggles, and each year presents new challenges. But each year also brings a new crop of gifted young women whose passion for computers and technology finds a natural outlet in the context of the SpelBots. And I'm praying for even greater opportunities to fulfill God's purpose for me in the future, whether it's at Spelman College or somewhere else.

Read the Directions

As I reflect on the storied history of African Americans who have been influential in science and technology, I continue to hear my call. Groundbreaking figures like George Washington Carver (botany), Charles Drew (cardiology), Percy Julian (chemistry), Henry Sampson (nuclear engineering), and Mark Dean (computer science) populate the annals of modern science. And all of them were "firsts" in some form or fashion. (Please, I encourage you to look them up.)

But, sadly, save for a few brilliant, modern-day trailblazers like robotics expert Dr. Ayanna Howard, formerly with NASA and now at the Georgia Institute of Technology, or Dr. Monica Anderson at the University of Alabama, the names of female computer scientists and roboticists, especially African American, are few and far between. If this is ever going to change, it must begin in grade school and continue through college. Young girls need to know that there is a place for them in these important fields. Who knows? One of them may be the next Bill Gates or Steve Jobs or Dr. Ben Carson. They may be research professors at MIT, rocket scientists at NASA, Web innovators at Google, or next generation iPhone inventors at Apple.

Sometimes, despite a person's gifts and abilities, people (and institutions) will find ways to box our young people into a predetermined category that says: "He's not the right kind of person for this job" or "She's just missing something."

There will be those who keep us in a box, but if we have talent and determination, the boxes can be overcome. However, if we don't at least get a complete education and put forth our best effort, then we have no one to blame but ourselves.

On the other hand, some young people hide in a box that they have designed to protect themselves from their fears and failure. Only when they learn to step out of that box can they begin to reach their full potential.

My hope is that more young people will see the connection between what they do, in school and how it affects everything that comes later, because once they do it can transform their vision for life. Indeed, it could be the difference between taking a summer job at a fast-food chain and making $6.55 an hour and working an internship at a technology firm and earning many times that amount by doing fun and creative things (like working on the next iPhone or doing a summer research experience at Carnegie Mellon or Georgia Tech and working on a humanoid robot or some other autonomous robot). Paying attention in school can bring huge economic dividends down the line. But more important, an education can make one a more complete and well-rounded person.

One of my great motivations as a teacher is the thought that, someday, one of the young women or men who sit in my classes could go on to create something miraculous that will change the world—something that will restore sight to the blind, repair our fragile environment, or reduce cancer to a beatable malady.

Really, the possibilities are wide open. But what troubles me is that many potential scientific breakthroughs are being missed because young people who have the imagination and aptitude to develop those innovative devices are dropping out of school or settling for a diploma when they should be pursuing their doctorates.

My call is to do everything I can to make sure none of those young people will miss their destiny. That none of them will wind up stuck in a self-imposed box of hopelessness or low expectations.

The phrase "out of the box" can also be a metaphor for that first moment when you take a robot kit out of its packaging, when all the different pieces are scattered and disconnected. Because those pieces make up a complex system, you need directions to assemble it into a functional whole. But sometimes the pieces don't seem to fit or they are defective. Sometimes the pieces need to be repaired. In the Bible, God gives us the directions we need to put our disconnected lives back together. As Pastor Terry Worthington, from back in my Free Methodist Church days, used to say, "If at first you don't succeed, read the directions." God is the master designer and engineer, and He didn't make us into artificially intelligent robots but rather living and breathing human beings in His own image—beings with the choice to love or hate, heal or hurt, serve or neglect.

Most important, He has given us the freedom to believe or reject His truth. And in my journey, I've learned it's always better to seek after and choose His truth. As we give our lives to God, He redeems our broken pieces and restores the function and beauty He intended to come out of the box.

Notes

1. AIBO stands for Artificial Intelligence roBOt; the acronym is homonymous with the Japanese term for "companion."
2. Quotes and S.H.A.P.E. acrostic from *The Purpose-Driven Life* by Rick Warren (Grand Rapids, Mich.: Zondervan, 2002), 241–48.
3. Statistics from "African Americans Studying STEM: Parsing the Numbers" by Anne Sasso, *Science* magazine, May 16, 2008, www.sciencemag.org.
4. From *Ebony* magazine, September 2005.
5. Find out more information at www.artsialliance.org.
6. Teach to encourage the body of Christ; Enable young African Americans to reach their full potential spiritually, academically, vocationally, and economically; Advertise the glory of God and the gospel; Create community; and Humbly learn from Christ.

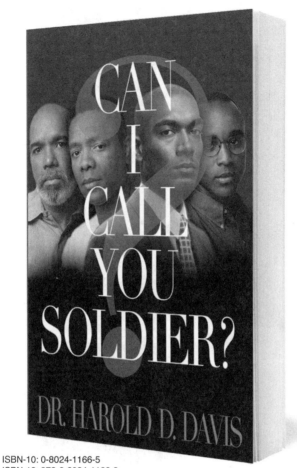

ISBN-10: 0-8024-1166-5
ISBN-13: 978-0-8024-1166-2

The war is at home and the battlefield is in the lives of our young men. In any community, and particularly in the black community, millions of young men feel the void of a role model. For every absent father, complacent leader, and passive bystander, there is a man who will step in and be a father figure—whether he is a trustworthy man of God or a dangerous enemy, someone will fill the void. It's up to us to win this battle and prepare the next generation to join in the fight. For the many men wondering how to win…*Can I Call You Soldier?* will be their strategy for victory.

by Dr. Harold D. Davis
Find it now at your favorite local or online bookstore.

www.LiftEveryVoiceBooks.com

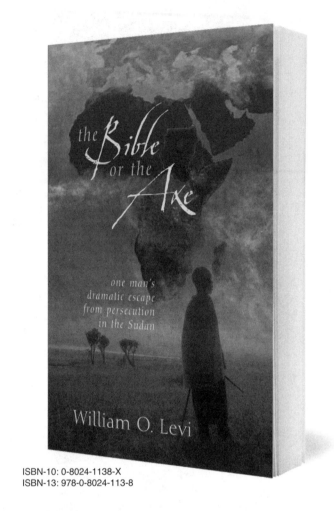

ISBN-10: 0-8024-1138-X
ISBN-13: 978-0-8024-113-8

Exile. Persecution. Torture. The riveting story of one man's escape from the Sudan. By the muddy banks of the Kulo-jobi River, a young Sudanese boy is faced with a decision that will shape the rest of his life.

William Levi was born in southern Sudan as part of a Messianic Hebrew tribal group and spent the majority of his growing up years as a refugee running from Islamic persecution. He was eventually taken captive for refusing to convert to Islam and suffered greatly at the hands of his captor

by William O. Levi

Find it now at your favorite local or online bookstore.

www.LiftEveryVoiceBooks.com

The Negro National Anthem

Lift every voice and sing
Till earth and heaven ring,
Ring with the harmonies of Liberty;
Let our rejoicing rise
High as the listening skies,
Let it resound loud as the rolling sea.
Sing a song, full of the faith that the dark past has taught us,
Sing a song, full of the hope that the present has brought us,
Facing the rising sun, of our new day begun
Let us march on till victory is won.

So begins the Black National Anthem, by James Weldon Johnson in 1900. Lift Every Voice is the name of the joint imprint of The Institute for Black Family Development and Moody Publishers.

Our vision is to advance the cause of Christ through publishing African-American Christians who educate, edify, and disciple Christians in the church community through quality books written for African-Americans.

Since 1988, the Institute for Black Family Development, a 501 (c) (3) nonprofit Christian organization, has been providing training and technical assistance for churches and Christian organizations. The Institute for Black Family Development's goal is to become a premier trainer in leadership development, management, and strategic planning for pastors, ministers, volunteers, executives, and key staff members of churches and Christian organizations. To learn more about The Institute for Black Family Development, write us at:

The Institute for Black Family Development
15151 Faust
Detroit, MI 48223

We hope you enjoy this book from Moody Publishers. Our goal is to provide high-quality, thought-provoking books and products that connect truth to your real needs and challenges. For more information on other books and products written and produced from a biblical perspective, go to www.moodypublishers.com or write to:

Moody Publishers/LEV
820 N. LaSalle Boulevard
Chicago, IL 60610
www.moodypublishers.com